As one of the world's longest established
and best-known travel brands,
Thomas Cook are the experts in travel.

For more than 135 years our
guidebooks have unlocked the secrets
of destinations around the world,
sharing with travellers a wealth of

GW00660429

Thomas Cook **pocket** guides

TOULOUSE
Jane Anson

Thomas
Cook

Your travelling companion since 1873

Written by Jane Anson

Published by Thomas Cook Publishing
A division of Thomas Cook Tour Operations Limited
Company registration No: 3772199 England
The Thomas Cook Business Park, 9 Coningsby Road
Peterborough PE3 8SB, United Kingdom
Email: books@thomascook.com, Tel: +44 (0)1733 416477
www.thomascookpublishing.com

Produced by The Content Works Ltd
Aston Court, Kingsmead Business Park, Frederick Place
High Wycombe, Bucks HP11 1LA
www.thecontentworks.com

Series design based on an original concept by Studio 183 Limited

ISBN: 978-1-84848-289-0

First edition © 2008 Thomas Cook Publishing
This second edition © 2010 Thomas Cook Publishing
Text © Thomas Cook Publishing
Maps © Thomas Cook Publishing/PCGraphics (UK) Limited
Transport map © Communicarta Limited

Series Editor: Kelly Pipes
Production/DTP: Steven Collins

Printed and bound in Spain by GraphyCems

Cover photography (Cassoulet de Toulouse) © Michael Brauner, Bon Appetit/Alamy

CONTENTS

INTRODUCING TOULOUSE
Introduction...6
When to go..8
Aeronautical Toulouse.................12
History 14
Lifestyle...16
Culture..18

MAKING THE MOST OF TOULOUSE
Shopping..22
Eating & drinking 24
Entertainment & nightlife............30
Sport & relaxation...........................34
Accommodation 36
The best of Toulouse.....................40
Suggested itineraries....................42
Something for nothing...................44
When it rains 46
On arrival 48

THE CITY OF TOULOUSE
The Old Town.....................................58
Île Ramier &
   the Left Bank 74
The Boulevards &
   further afield...............................86

OUT OF TOWN TRIPS
The Pyrénées 102
The Vineyards 114

PRACTICAL INFORMATION
Directory..126
Emergencies 136

INDEX 138

MAPS
Toulouse..50
Toulouse transport map.............54
The Old Town....................................60
Île Ramier &
   the Left Bank 76
The Boulevards &
   further afield 88
Around Toulouse..........................104

POCKET GUIDES

SYMBOLS KEY

The following symbols are used throughout this book:

ⓐ address ☎ telephone 🅦 website address ⓔ email
🕒 opening times 🆁 public transport connections ❶ important

The following symbols are used on the maps:

ℹ️ information office
✈ airport
➕ hospital
🚔 police station
🚌 bus station
🚉 railway station
Ⓜ metro
✝ cathedral
❶ numbers denote featured cafés & restaurants

▨ points of interest
○ city
○ large town
○ small town
═ motorway
— main road
— minor road
— railway

Hotels and restaurants are graded by approximate price as follows:
£ budget price **££** mid-range price **£££** expensive

Abbreviations used in addresses:

av.   avenue
blvd   boulevard
pl.   place (square)

▶ *The Capitole, Toulouse's 250-year-old Town Hall*

CAPITOLIUM

INTRODUCING
Toulouse

Introduction

There are some French cities that feel very much part of northern Europe – say Paris, Lille, or Bordeaux – and are all about elegance and sophistication. There are others – Lyon, Marseille, and very definitely Toulouse – that belong to southern Europe and the Mediterranean.

◆ *Place du Capitole's grand Town Hall in the heart of Toulouse*

Even the nickname of Toulouse, La Ville Rose, or 'pink city', conjures up images of lazy sunshine and laid back beauty. The name actually comes from the local red clay which the Romans used to build the city, although most of the handsome red brick you can see today dates back to the 15th century.

In terms of economy and size, however, Toulouse is anything but lazy and laid back. Toulouse is the capital of the Midi-Pyrénées, the largest region in metropolitan France. It has 120,000 students, the biggest student population in the country after Paris. And with well over a million inhabitants, the city is the fourth biggest in France.

More importantly, Toulouse is also the fastest growing city in Europe. Aviation and spaceflight have transformed the economy. Almost 10 per cent of the population work in the civil aviation and space industries, in particular Airbus and the Space City initiative.

Toulouse's location in the southwest of France, near the Pyrénées mountains and the Spanish border and not far from the Languedoc and the Côte d'Azur, translates into a relaxed, culturally rich lifestyle. The city heaves with late night bars and restaurants, street markets and festivals. As the préfecture (capital) of the Haute-Garonne region it is the unofficial centre of Occitan culture, and many of the festivals revolve around this colourful, passionate and historic community. With all this going on, you can safely come here expecting a lively, vibrant city full of concerts, culture, and good food, wine and weather.

When to go

Toulouse is a top destination at any time of year. In the heat of summer, life moves outdoors, into parks, onto terrace restaurants and bars. You can take boat trips on the Canal du Midi or pop to the coastline for some beach indulgence. In winter, Toulouse's location close to the Pyrénées makes it a great base for adventurous weekend sports. Costs don't vary on- and off-peak as much as in some cities, although in summer it is best to book well in advance.

SEASONS & CLIMATE

The weather is welcoming most of the year. Spring begins in March or April, with temperatures climbing to around 20°C (68°F). July and August are very hot, with an average temperature of 28°C (82°F) and over ten hours of sunshine per day. Autumn is often rainy, but still warm. Snow has been known in winter, but it is rarely freezing.

ANNUAL EVENTS

Toulouse is a city that likes to celebrate, and you'll often find yourself in the middle of a festival. The large number of students means that many events are centred on contemporary culture, from film festivals to live music gigs.

January–February
Contemporary Dance Festival Featuring international companies and young artists. ● (05) 61 59 98 78 Ⓦ www.cdctoulouse.com

Zoom Arrière Festival rediscovering forgotten film classics. ⓐ 69 rue du Taur ⓣ (05) 62 30 30 10 ⓦ www.lacinemathequedetoulouse.com ⓥ Metro: Capitole

March–April

Flamenco Festival This feast of Andalusian music and dancing takes place over ten days in late April. ⓣ (05) 34 25 81 21 ⓦ www.festival-flamenco-toulouse.com

Le Printemps du Rire Festival of stand-up comedy, theatre and improvisation. ⓣ (05) 62 21 23 24 ⓦ www.printempsdurire.com

▲ *Aerial view of the city and the Canal du Midi*

May–June

Le Marathon des Mots Free street theatre throughout the city, plus ticketed plays, readings, concerts and dance productions. ❶ (05) 61 99 64 01 Ⓦ www.lemarathondesmots.com

Rio Loco International world music festival focused on a different country each year. ❸ Prairie des Filtres rue Laganne ❶ (05) 61 32 77 28 Ⓝ Metro: Esquirol Ⓦ www.rio-loco.org

July–August

Dance Festival Contemporary dance events during the first week of July. ❶ (05) 62 30 69 10 Ⓦ www.jamescarles.com

Toulouse In Summer Over 400 musicians give concerts, often free, at the major parks, galleries and monuments around Toulouse. Expect anything from jazz, rock, tango or hip hop to classical and opera. ❶ (05) 62 27 60 60 Ⓦ www.mairie-toulouse.fr

September–October

Visual Arts Festival Also known as Les Printemps de Septembre (Springtime in September), a free festival dedicated to visual arts of all types. ❶ (05) 34 51 39 85 Ⓦ www.printempsdeseptembre.com

Festival de Rue de Ramonville September street party around Place Jean-Jaurès. ❶ (05) 61 73 00 48 Ⓝ Metro: Jean-Jaurès Ⓦ www.festivalramonville-arto.fr

November–December

Short Film Festival Festival of award-winning short films and children's films. ❶ (05) 61 11 02 22 Ⓦ www.toulouse-tourisme.com

Toulouse Antiques Fair One of France's biggest and best antiques fairs with over 300 dealers descending on the city in November.

🔵 Parc des Expositions de Toulouse, Rond point Michel Bénech
🔵 www.salon-antiquaires-toulouse.com 🔵 10.00–19.00
🔵 Metro: Les Arènes. Admission charge
Marché de Noel Christmas market with over 130 stands
of presents, decorations and festive food. 🔵 Pl. du Capitole
🔵 (05) 61 52 74 21 🔵 Metro: Capitole

PUBLIC HOLIDAYS
Jour de l'An (New Year's Day) 1 Jan
Lundi de Pâques (Easter Monday) 13 Apr 2010, 25 Apr 2011,
10 Apr 2012
Fête du Travail (Labour Day) 1 May
Victoire 1945 (World War II Armistice) 8 May
Ascension 13 May 2010, 2 June 2011, 17 May 2012
Lundi de Pentecôte (Whit Monday) 24 May 2010, 13 June
2011, 28 May 2012
Bastille Day/Fête Nationale (French Revolution) 14 July
Assomption (Assumption) 15 Aug
Touissant (All Saints Day) 1 Nov
Armistice 1918 (World War I Armistice) 11 Nov
Noël (Christmas Day) 25 Dec

On public holidays government departments, banks, shops
and even some restaurants are closed. If a public holiday falls
on a Thursday or a Tuesday, many French like to *faire le pont*
(bridge over) and take a four-day weekend.

Aeronautical Toulouse

For the past few centuries, Toulouse has been all about flying –
both on earth and in space – and today it is one of France's most
high tech cities.

Clement Adler, the first human to fly in an aircraft powered
by a motor, was born in Muret, 20 km from Toulouse. He worked
as an engineer in the city, experimenting at the end of the 19th
century with machines that flapped their wings like birds. He
eventually managed to get 15 cm (6 in) off the ground in 1886
in a bat-shaped monoplane called *L'École* (the School).

Rather more successfully, Toulouse later became the base of
the first regular airline taking off from French soil. Pierre-Georges
Latécoère (founder of France's first regular mail and passenger
plane in the 1930s), the fighter pilot Jean Daurat, the heroic Jean

Mermoz and the writer and pilot Antoine de Saint-Exupéry all have strong links with the city.

Today, Toulouse is the centre of the European aerospace industry. Alcatel Alenia Space, EADS Astrium, and Galileo have a significant presence in Toulouse, and the headquarters of Airbus SAS has been based here since the 1970s. Almost 12,000 people are employed by Airbus in Toulouse, and you can take tours of its iconic planes, including the new double decker A300. You can also walk onboard the last model of Concorde (see page 92).

In 1997 Toulouse saw the launch of a space-themed adventure park, the Cité de l'Espace (see page 90). Here you can see a recreation of the MIR Space Station, the Sputnik 1 satellite and the Ariane 5 Rocket, as well as watch movies at an IMAX cinema.

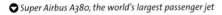
● *Super Airbus A380, the world's largest passenger jet*

History

As with many big cities, Toulouse's location and its wide, navigable river were responsible for its early rise to prominence. The River Garonne was forded in the 8th century BC, and the area became a focal point for trade between the Pyrénées, the Mediterranean and the Atlantic. A large fertile plain north of the city meant that locals could farm and grow food. It was known as *Tolosa*, a name that has remained practically unchanged over the centuries, despite various invasions by the Celts, the Romans and the Visigoths.

The Romans arrived in 125 BC, founding the nearby Narbonne. Toulouse enjoyed a fruitful relationship with them, at first simply as allies. Inevitably, when Julius Caesar arrived and took control of Gaul, Toulouse became part of the Roman Empire. The city moved to its current position, built walls around its border as a symbol of imperial favour, and became one of the most powerful cities in the empire. It was filled with popular baths, aqueducts, circuses, theatres, a forum, and a sophisticated sewage system. The Saint Sernin basilica, today one of Toulouse's most visited and beautiful local attractions, was founded in memory of the city's first Christian bishop, who was martyred on the site.

The Visigoths, who took over the city after the Romans in the 5th century, realised what a treasure they had. Give or take one or two invasions, things ran smoothly and successfully for Toulouse. From the 9th to the 13th centuries, Toulouse was the seat of one of the most beautiful courts of Europe. A refined civilisation and culture developed, giving birth to such things as the literature of the Langue d'Oc, and the *troubadours*, wandering musicians who travelled the country composing and playing their music. The city officially became part of France in 1271.

The Inquisition had a big effect on Toulouse, and for almost 400 years the city was the centre of the Inquisition in southern France. Countless heretics were burned at the stake. The city remained economically successful, thanks to the popularity of its local fabric dye, woad, and many of the large properties and public buildings that dominate the downtown area today were built during this time. In a bright moment, the University was also founded. Toulouse remained relatively independent until the French Revolution in 1789.

Toulouse's luck held out after the Revolution as well, paradoxically in the fact that it missed many of the industrial developments of the 19th century. Unlike so many cities, this means that there are now very few ugly industrial factories in the downtown area, and many historic monuments are still fully intact.

The city enjoyed strong development in the last decades of the 20th century, in part due to the civil aviation industry and National Space Centre. Despite a momentary slow-down during the global crisis of 2009, Toulouse's economy looks set, once again, to rocket.

● *Ready for lift-off!*

Lifestyle

Southern France is known for its relaxed lifestyle, and Toulouse is no exception. People like to work fewer hours and enjoy themselves more. Their laid back, welcoming attitude extends to visitors. Even at sporting events rivalry is friendly rather than fierce, and you'll often hear Toulouse fans singing the opposing team's songs to keep the atmosphere sweet. The large number of visiting students also contributes to the feel of a thriving, international city. Most weekends you'll find a celebration or festival going on.

Restaurants tend to serve lunch between 12.00 and 14.00, and dinner between 19.00 and 22.00, but you'll find more exceptions to this rule than in many French cities. Most restaurant staff are very relaxed with children, and you will often see families eating together in the evening.

CANAL DU MIDI

This 240 km World Heritage classified canal stretches from above Toulouse right down to Sète. Originally conceived as a shortcut between the Atlantic and the Mediterranean, it has 103 locks and countless bridges, dams and a tunnel. It snakes around the city of Toulouse. To see it at its best, cross the Jardin Japonais, part of the Jardin Compans Caffarelli (see page 91), stroll along to the Port de l'Embouchure and take a boat trip up to the lock gates. Boat trips are available from NaviCanal (see page 56).

● *Peacefully meandering down the Canal du Midi*

As with anywhere in France, it is appreciated if you try to speak a bit of the language. Many people do speak English but it does pay to greet shopkeepers and restaurant owners with a *bonjour* and *s'il vous plaît*.

Throughout its history Toulouse has been a highly religious city, and this is still true today. Largely Catholic, there are numerous religious festivals and active churches all over the city. If you would like to attend a service try the Saint Sernin basilica (see page 58), one of the best examples of a Roman church in the country, or Saint Pierre des Cuisines (see page 63), the oldest religious building in Toulouse. Be aware that, partly as a result of this strong Catholicism in the city, almost everything is closed on Sundays.

Culture

Toulouse is a young, vibrant, international city. It is filled with students from all over the world, and with high tech international companies employing young and ambitious staff. As a result, the city is heaving with arts and culture all year round, from theatre and music to street art and dance. Visiting groups come regularly, drawn by the 15 large scale festivals throughout the year.

Big-name international musicians generally play at the Zénith stadium, which seats an audience of 9,000 (see page 85). Oasis, for example, was one of several famous bands who performed here in 2009. Concerts by local musicians and sporting events also take place at the stadium. Classical music is regularly performed at the **Théâtre du Capitole** (ⓐ Pl. du Capitole ❶ (05) 61 63 13 13 ⓦ www.theatre-du-capitole.org), and some of the best concerts you will hear are of classical piano, organ or string music, often beautifully staged among the city's many historical monuments. Smaller theatre workshops and concerts spring up regularly in arts theatres and bars everywhere. There are festivals all year round, adding to the feeling that this is a city embracing its cultural heritage.

The rich cultural life of this southwest city is easily seen by the wide range of excellent museums on offer, many housed in the historical buildings that criss-cross the downtown area. One museum not to miss is Musée des Augustins (see page 66) with paintings and sculpture dating back to the Middle Ages

◗ *The Capitole's stunning reception hall, the Salles des Illustres*

and a wonderful adjoining convent.

As you will soon notice, however, art and culture in Toulouse span a very wide spectrum, and it is not so much medieval museums as contemporary artworks that really make the city stand out. There is a thriving graffiti scene that has, controversially, become famous across Europe. Look out for sloe-eyed nymph girls in provocative poses, drawn by the notorious Miss Van of the graffiti artist club Hanky Panky Girls. Miss Van now lives in Barcelona and exhibits in galleries across Europe and in New York, but her influence in her hometown of Toulouse is still huge and there are dozens of young graffiti artists hoping to follow in her high-heeled footsteps. Along the quays are dozens of free galleries showcasing the latest works from young artists, while the more established talents make it into Les Abattoirs (see page 79), a contemporary art space that has revitalised an entire section of the Left Bank of the city.

There's always something going on in Toulouse, from festivals and concerts to theatre performances and special exhibitions, so it's worth finding out what's on during your stay. Before you arrive, check the tourist information website (see page 134), which has a useful searchable calendar of forthcoming cultural events. You can pick up the free magazines *Toulouse Cultures* and *Les Clés de L'Art* at the tourist office or at your hotel, or purchase the comprehensive *Toulouse Flashebdo* for a small fee at any newsstand. Some big-name performances get quickly sold out, so purchase tickets online via **FNAC** (ⓦ www.fnacspectacles.com) and collect them when you arrive.

▶ *A heady mix of architectural styles in central Toulouse*

MAKING THE MOST OF
Toulouse

Shopping and food make a good combination in Toulouse. The city is heaving with excellent markets, upmarket delicatessens, bakeries and *épiceries* (grocery stores). Head to the covered Victor Hugo market (see page 68) for locally produced *foie gras*, cheeses, charcuteries, and of course the best Toulouse sausage you can buy. There are lots of good food and wine shops around the outside, plus small eateries on the first floor. Don't forget to pop into a *cave à vins* (wine cellar – two of the best are actually stalls within Victor Hugo market) and get some expert advice on the region's local wines.

Shopping and clothes are also well matched here. The large department stores **Galeries Lafayette** (ⓐ 77 rue Alsace Lorraine) and **Nouvelles Galeries** (ⓐ 4–8 rue Lapeyrouse) are handy, but for original designer clothes and shoes concentrate on the chic streets between Place President Wilson, Place St Georges and the Musée des Augustins. There are also a number of quirky vintage clothes shops.

Rue Croix Baragnon and the small streets around the Place Saint-Etienne are the best places to find trendy interior design shops, with anything from lamps to rugs to sculptures.

Books and records are easy to find around Place du Capitole. Besides a number of very well stocked libraries, Toulouse boasts an impressive *médiathèque* (see page 95).

If you're looking for an indoor shopping centre, head for Carrefour at Portet-sur-Garonne (see page 97), or St Georges, near Place St Georges.

USEFUL SHOPPING PHRASES

What time do the shops (this shop) open/close?
A quelle heure ouvrent/ferment les magasins
(ce magasin)?
*Ah kel ur oovra / fairm lay magazahn
(suh magazahn)?*

How much is this?
Ça fait combien?
Sa fay kombyen?

Do you take credit cards?
Prenez-vous les cartes de crédit?
Pruhnay voo lay kart duh kraydee?

My size is...
Ma taille est...
Ma tie eh...

I'll take this one, thank you
Je prends celui-ci/celle-ci merci
Juh prohn selwee-see / sell see mehrsee

Can I try this on?
Puis-je essayer ceci?
Pwee juh ehssayeh suhsee?

Eating & drinking

Toulouse is a city for gourmets. As in much of southwest France, one of the key local specialities is duck. You can gorge yourself on *foie gras*, the controversial fattened duck liver paté that is not for the delicate-hearted, as well as *rillettes* (a coarser duck paté), hearty duck soups and potatoes sautéed in duck fat. Markets have an endless variety of these products and many will offer free samples.

Local cheese is also good. Try *brebis*, sheep's milk cheese from the nearby Pyrénées mountains, often laced with spices or even local liqueurs. Toulouse's river, canal and location between the Atlantic and the Mediterranean mean that many bistros do wonderful seafood platters, with everything from lobster to tiny *boulots* (periwinkles).

The local vineyards add colour and warmth to your meal, and as many are close to the city, it is worth taking a day trip out to discover some local producers (see page 114). There are

PRICE CATEGORIES

Based on the average price per head for a two-course dinner, excluding drinks. Lunch will usually be cheaper, and most restaurants offer a very good value *prix fixe* (set menu) option at lunchtime.

£ up to €18   ££ €18–30   £££ over €30

● *Pavement cafés, perfect for watching the world go by*

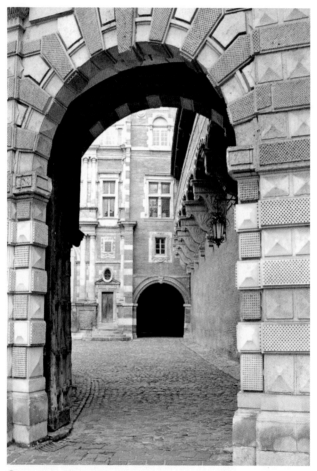

�l View through an archway into a courtyard in central Toulouse

CASSOULET

Cassoulet is the most famous of Toulouse dishes. It is a rich, slow-cooked bean casserole containing meat (typically pork sausages, mutton or duck), *couennes* (pork skin) and white haricot beans. The dish is named after the *cassole*, the distinctive oval covered earthenware pot in which cassoulet is traditionally cooked. It is traditional to use the pot from the previous cassoulet in order to give a base for the next one – in theory just having one endless pot on the go. You'll find many restaurants, both in Toulouse and the surrounding areas, that have their own versions of the dish. In the city centre, **La Cave au Cassoulet** (📍 54 rue Peyrolières ☎ (05) 61 13 60 30) claims to make the most authentic version.

a number of good traditional wine merchants, plus two stalls in Victor Hugo market which provide local bottles. The student population also ensures there are plenty of beer joints, cocktail bars and wine bars, many around Place du Capitole and Rue Gambetta.

Local food intermingles with international cuisine and the city has literally thousands of cafés, bars, pizzerias, oriental and other international eateries. The more upmarket restaurants are concentrated around Place President Wilson and Place du Capitole, while smaller neighbourhood favourites can be found in the narrow streets leading down to the Garonne river around Pont Neuf or in Saint Cyprien. For something different,

USEFUL DINING PHRASES

I would like a table for ... people
Je voudrais une table pour ... personnes
Juh voodray oon tabl poor ... pehrson

Waiter/waitress
Monsieur/mademoiselle (the traditional term
garçon is no longer considered polite)
M'syer/madmwahzel

May I have the bill please?
L'addition, s'il vous plaît
L'adission, sill voo play

Could I have this rare/medium/well cooked
Je le voudrais saignant/à point/bien cuit
Juh luh voodray saynyohn/ah pwan/bi-yen kwee

I am vegetarian
Je suis végétarien/végétarienne
Juh swee vehjaytaryan/vehjaytaryen

Where are the toilets please?
Où sont les toilettes s'il vous plaît?
Oo son lay twahlet, sill voo play?

Can I see the wine list?
La carte des vins s'il vous plaît
Lah cart day vahn sill voo play

try **L'Occitania** (ⓐ L'Ecluse Bayard ⓣ (05) 61 63 06 06
ⓦ www.loccitania.fr), a floating restaurant moored on
the Canal du Midi.

Restaurant bills are almost always *service compris* (service
included), so tipping or rounding up is an extra to acknowledge
good service. Major credit cards are accepted pretty much
everywhere, although you might need cash for the smaller
fast-food joints and kebab shops.

Since January 2008, smoking has been banned in all public
spaces, including restaurants and bars.

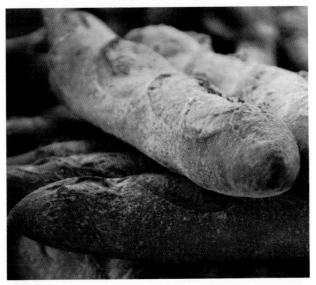

🔺 *Du pain, s'il vous plaît*

Entertainment & nightlife

Toulouse's nightlife is lively, constantly changing and evolving. You'll find plenty to do just by wandering around and stumbling on bars, theatres and clubs, particularly around the Place du Capitole. If you like to plan, local listings magazines include the free *Toulouse Cultures, Les Clés de L'Art* and the good value *Toulouse Flashebdo*. These are available from the tourist office, magazine stands and some hotels.

There are five main theatres in the city as well as countless smaller establishments. Try the traditional Théâtre Garonne (see page 82) or the more avant-garde **Nouveau Théâtre Jules-Julien** (ⓐ 6 av. des Écoles Jules-Julien ⓣ (05) 61 25 79 92). For classical music, head to the Théâtre du Capitole (see page 18). The Halle aux Grains (see page 94) has a mix of classical and modern music, plus contemporary dance. The **Église St Pierre des Chartreux** (ⓐ 21 rue Valade ⓣ (05) 61 21 99 34) is a picturesque scene for concerts staged throughout the year, from organ recitals to local choirs. The music scene gets distinctly hipper at newer spaces such as **Salle Nougaro** (ⓐ 20 chemin du Garric ⓣ (05) 61 93 79 40 ⓦ www.sallenougaro.com), where alternative musicians congregate.

There are bars everywhere around Place du Capitole, Place Saint Georges, Place President Wilson and Rue de Metz. For an edgier feel, head for emerging areas such as the far side of Pont Neuf, around Rue de la République, or the roads around the Grand Rond. The Stade Municipal (see page 34) often

ⓓ *Place du Capitole by night*

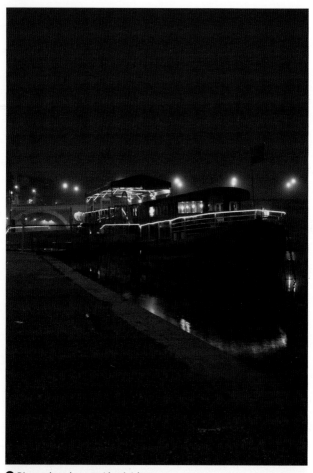

◆ *Dinner aboard a quayside péniche*

welcomes big international names and many bars and restaurants have live music.

Expect the drinking and dancing to go on until late, with most places staying open until 02.00 or 03.00. Good bars include Le Zénith and Chapeau Rouge (see page 85). For clubbers, there are frequent DJ nights at Parc Expo (see page 85). Experimental club music, including punk, disco and house, can be found at Le Kléo/Le Ramier nightclub on the Île du Ramier (see page 85).

In summer, even when the bars have closed up for the night, life moves out onto the streets. Around the Pont Neuf bridge and other open spaces, you can join late night revellers chatting, dancing, or cramming into the few small clubs and bars that remain open until dawn.

And if you're over 21 and looking to burn some cash, there's also a large casino, the Salies-du-Salat (see page 100), with over 120 slot machines, four roulette tables, a restaurant and a piano bar.

Film fanatics have plenty of options, and many of the local cinemas screen English language films. *Version originale* (VO) means a screening in the original language, with subtitles. Around Place du Capitole, you'll find the Cinémathèque (see page 63), **ABC** (ⓐ 13 rue Saint-Bernard ⓦ www.abc-toulouse.net) and **Utopia Toulouse** (ⓐ 24 rue Montardy ⓦ www.cinemas-utopia.org/toulouse). You could also try **Cratère Toulouse** (ⓐ 95 grand rue Saint-Michel ⓦ www.cinemalecratere.com) or **Mega CGR** (ⓐ Centre Commercial Leclerc Blagnac ⓦ www.cgrcinemas.fr). For arty cinema, make the trek to **Ramonville** (ⓐ l'Autan ⓣ (05) 61 73 89 03) and **Auzielle** (ⓐ Studio 7 ⓣ (05) 61 39 02 37).

Sport & relaxation

Toulouse is a healthy city of green spaces, clear rivers and great footpaths. Rugby is by far the biggest spectator sport, and locals are fiercely proud of both their team and the fact that Toulouse hosted games for the Rugby World Cup 2007.

SPECTATOR SPORTS

Stade Municipal de Toulouse Nicknamed *Le TéFéCé*, or *Les Violets* for their purple shirts, the local football team Toulouse FC is becoming increasingly successful. The stadium has a capacity of over 35,000 and was one of the key stages in the 1998 FIFA World Cup. **ⓐ** 1 allée Gabriel Biénès, Île du Ramier **ⓣ** 0892 700 831 **ⓦ** www.tfc.info **ⓝ** Bus: 12, 52

Stade Toulousain The biggest rugby matches are played at the Stade Municipal de Toulouse (see above), although the team's home stadium has recently been renovated and can hold almost 20,000 spectators. **ⓐ** Stade Ernest Wallen, 114 rue Troènes **ⓣ** 08 92 69 31 15 **ⓦ** www.stadetoulousain.fr **ⓝ** Metro: Arènes

PARTICIPATION

L'Aeroclub Air France de Toulouse Established aeronautical club. **ⓐ** 4 av. Jean-René Lagasse, Balma **ⓣ** (05) 61 34 85 11 **ⓦ** www.acaf-toulouse.com

Bicycle hire Movimento offer bicycle hire with outlets at the Square du Général Charles de Gaulle, the bus station, and Port Saint Sauveur. **ⓐ** 5 Port Saint Sauveur **ⓣ** (05) 34 30 03 00 **ⓛ** 10.30–13.00, 14.00–18.40 Mon–Sat **ⓝ** Bus: 22 to Port Saint-Etienne

Elastic Jump Most bungee jumping takes place near Castres, about 90 minutes away. ⓐ 1 chemin de Castillon, Pechbonnieu ⓣ (05) 61 74 64 00 ⓦ www.elasticjump.com

Swimming Complex of indoor and outdoor swimming pools on Ramier Island. The real discovery is the Parc des Sports Summer Pool, with its rockeries and 1950s architecture. ⓐ Allée Gabriel-Biénès ⓣ (05) 61 22 31 35 ⓛ Indoor pool: 09.00–19.00 (school holidays); 16.00–19.00 Mon–Fri, 10.00–12.30, 15.00–19.00 Sat & Sun (rest of year); outdoor pool: 09.00–20.00, late June–Aug; 09.00–19.00, Sept; times vary so always phone ahead ⓝ Bus: 12

RELAXATION

Yoga School Toulouse Introductory hours available.
ⓐ 46 rue de Metz ⓣ (05) 61 25 17 69 ⓦ www.yogaetmeditation.fr
ⓛ Call ahead for class times ⓝ Metro: Capitole

🔺 *La Garonne, for leisurely strolling, sightseeing and boating*

Accommodation

It is easy to find good value basic accommodation in Toulouse, but less easy to find luxury. There are just three 4-star hotels, none of which really compete with their equivalents in Paris or London. There are a number of good small hotels and hostels, however, and several apartments to rent.

Check-in and check-out times are usually fairly relaxed. Breakfast is often extra, and can be expensive, so you might want to skip it and head to one of the many coffee shops around the city. Some hotel rates vary during the busy summer months, but largely speaking prices don't fluctuate too much in high season.

Toulouse accommodation online Ⓦ www.toulouse-tourisme.com/hebergement

Hotel bookings and availability hotline ❶ 08 92 70 02 97

HOTELS

Hôtel Anatole France £ Simple hotel near Place du Capitole, with parking spaces. ❸ 46 pl. Anatole France (The Old Town) ❶ (05) 61 23 19 96 Ⓦ www.hotel-anatolefrance.com Ⓝ Metro: Capitole

PRICE CATEGORIES
Based on the average price for a double room for one night.
£ up to €45 **££** €45–80 **£££** over €80

Hôtel de Brienne ££ Just next to the canal on a tree-lined street, this is a modern, functional and inexpensive hotel. ⓐ 20 blvd du Maréchal Leclerc (The Boulevards & further afield) ⓣ (05) 61 23 60 60 ⓦ www.hoteldebrienne.com ⓝ Metro: Compans Caffarelli

Hôtel Heliot ££ A simple 12-room hotel close to Place President Wilson. Free wireless internet access. ⓐ 3 rue Heliot (The Old Town) ⓣ (05) 34 41 39 41 ⓦ www.hotel-heliot.com ⓝ Metro: Jean-Jaurès

Hôtel Mermoz ££ A lovely garden and wide terrace give this hotel an extra cachet. Free WiFi. ⓐ 50 rue Matabiau (The Boulevards & further afield) ⓣ (05) 61 63 04 04 ⓦ www.hotel-mermoz.com ⓝ Metro: Jean-Jaurès

Hôtel Saint Sernin ££ No prizes for guessing the location of this hotel. Ask for a room with a view of the basilica. ⓐ 2 rue Saint Bernard (The Old Town) ⓣ (05) 61 21 73 08 ⓦ www.hotelstsernin.com ⓝ Metro: Capitole

Hôtel du Taur ££ Well placed high above the Place du Capitole, with all bedrooms overlooking a quiet central courtyard. ⓐ 2 rue du Taur (The Old Town) ⓣ (05) 61 21 17 54 ⓦ www.hotel-du-taur.com ⓝ Metro: Capitole

Hôtel des Beaux Arts ££–£££ A fantastic small hotel, perfectly located by Pont Neuf, with many rooms offering views of the river. The rooms are small but well decorated. An excellent bistro is attached, where hotel guests receive a free glass of champagne.

📍 1 pl. du Pont Neuf (The Old Town) ☎ (05) 34 45 42 42
🌐 www.hoteldesbeauxarts.com Ⓜ Metro: Esquirol

Crowne Plaza £££ Comfortable and well located business hotel, with WiFi access, a gym and sauna. 📍 7 pl. du Capitole (The Old Town) ☎ (05) 61 61 19 13 🌐 www.crowne-plaza-toulouse.com
Ⓜ Metro: Capitole

Grand Hôtel de l'Opéra £££ The *grande dame* of Toulouse hotels, with the best location. Slightly stuffy, but very comfortable and good facilities. 📍 1 pl. du Capitole (The Old Town) ☎ (05) 61 21 82 66
🌐 www.grand-hotel-opera.com Ⓜ Metro: Capitole

Hôtel Garonne £££ Probably the smartest boutique hotel in town, this has a Japanese feel, lovely dark woods in the bedrooms and communal areas, and one of the city's best restaurants, called simply '19', directly opposite. Internet in all rooms. 📍 22 descente de la Halle aux Poissons (The Old Town)
☎ (05) 34 31 94 80 🌐 www.hotelgaronne.com Ⓜ Metro: Esquirol

APARTMENTS
Résidence les Princes £ Short-stay apartments for rent in a pretty red-bricked building, not far from La Halle aux Grains with its many concerts. Book well in advance, as there aren't many available. 📍 6 rue des Princes (The Boulevards & further afield)
☎ (05) 61 80 79 38 🌐 www.residencelesprinces.com Ⓜ Bus: 16, 22

HOSTELS & CAMPSITES
Camping de Rupé £ About 7 km out of the town centre, a very

🔺 *Pont Neuf, Toulouse's oldest bridge*

popular campsite that can get very lively over the summer months. ⓐ 21 chemin du Pont-de-Rupé (The Boulevards & further afield) ⓣ (05) 61 70 07 35 Ⓜ Bus: 59 from Place Jeanne d'Arc

Résidence Jolimont £ A fairly large hostel, with beds for up to 100 people. Most rooms have two beds. ⓐ 2 Av Yves Brunaud (The Boulevards & further afield) ⓣ (05) 34 30 42 80 Ⓦ www.residence-jolimont.com Ⓜ Metro: Jolimont

THE BEST OF TOULOUSE

Toulouse is a fairly compact city, so it is easy and fun to visit the key sites, even on a flying visit.

TOP 10 ATTRACTIONS

- **Eat cassoulet** Try the most famous local dish, ideally made with Toulouse sausage (see page 27)

- **The weir over the Garonne** Best viewed from the walkway behind Les Abattoirs Museum of Modern Art (see page 79)

- **Culture fix** Toulouse is packed full of art galleries, historical buildings and fabulous churches. Don't miss the Musée des Augustins (see page 66) and the Saint Sernin basilica (see page 58)

- **Victor Hugo market** A great place to spend a few hours. Lots of good food and wine shops around the outside, as well as a host of fascinating market stands (see page 45)

- **Canal du Midi** Rent a barge and cruise down the canal (see page 16)

- **Pont Neuf** Cross over and visit the Château d'Eau photography gallery (see page 81)

- **Jardin des Plantes** The Botanical Gardens are a great spot to hang out, and perfect for children to enjoy horse rides around the park (see page 62)

- **Ariège valley** Heading further out towards the Pyrénées, this unspoilt region is great for adventure sports (see page 109)

- **Chic shopping** Concentrate on the trendy streets that run between Place President Wilson, Place St Georges and the Musée des Augustins (see page 22)

- **Cité de l'Espace** Discover the high tech side of the city at this space-themed amusement park (see page 90)

❤ Much of Toulouse is prettily illuminated at night

Suggested itineraries

HALF-DAY: TOULOUSE IN A HURRY

Cram a feast of architecture, history and art into a few hours at one of Toulouse's most fabulous art galleries, the Musée des Augustins (see page 66). Then wander down to Place President Wilson and tackle a traditional cassoulet.

1 DAY: TIME TO SEE A LITTLE MORE

Grab a more contemporary art fix at Les Abattoirs (see page 79) or the Château d'Eau photography gallery (see page 81) on the far side of the Pont Neuf, Toulouse's oldest bridge. Lunch at the classic Jardins de l'Opéra (see page 72). Pick up a bargain from around Place St Georges, then finish with a walk along the Garonne river and dinner at the Brasserie des Beaux-Arts (see page 72).

2–3 DAYS: TIME TO SEE MUCH MORE

As well as the must-see traditional art, visit trendier galleries such as the Halle aux Poissons (see page 64). It's worth the trek to the Cité de l'Espace (see page 90) or the Airbus site (see page 92) for some high tech wonder. You can relax by the Garonne river and at the Jardin des Plantes (see page 62).

LONGER: ENJOYING TOULOUSE TO THE FULL

Toulouse's surrounding towns and villages are packed with possibilities. If you have time, visit Albi (see page 116) and Gaillac (see page 120) or, depending on the season, go skiing or hiking in the mountains (see page 108).

🔺 *Inside Les Jacobins, one of the city's most striking interiors*

Something for nothing

You don't need wads of cash to see the best of Toulouse. The city has a thousand hectares of green space – 160 parks, gardens and ancient brick-walled cloisters open free to the public. Add the footpaths along the Canal du Midi and the Garonne River

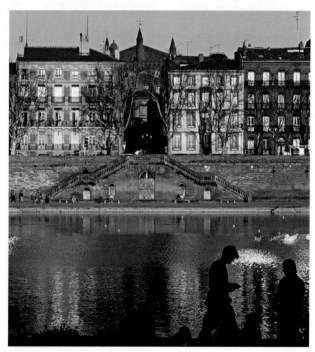

⬥ *Smart townhouses overlooking the Quai de Tounis*

and you can spend your whole holiday walking, wandering and wondering. The Botanical Gardens (see page 62) are especially good for children, with pony rides and grass track biking, although there is a charge for these.

The Chaussée de Bazacle gives the best free view of Toulouse, with water cascading over a weir at one of the widest points of the river. Or head to the other side of the river for EDF Bazacle (see page 63), an exhibition space in a hydroelectric power station where photographers regularly display their talent.

Art is open to all in Toulouse. Visit photo galleries such as Galerie de la Halle aux Poissons (see page 64) for free, and don't ignore the fabulous street art graffiti around the city. Increasingly, it is the underground that has been attracting some of the most exciting artists, with many metro stations exhibiting contemporary sculptures and paintings. Even the art galleries that charge admission are free on the first Sunday of every month. Striking architecture is free to admire in churches such as **Les Jacobins** (ⓦ www.jacobins.mairie-toulouse.fr ⏱ 09.00–19.00), with its 22 m (72 ft) columns supporting a giant arched roof.

The best day to be in town is Sunday, when the city centre is closed to cars and there are small street markets and free entertainment. Pick up a bargain at the Sunday morning flea market around the Saint Sernin basilica (see page 58) or buy a picnic from the St Aubin farmers' market.

The bustling fruit and vegetable markets Marché Victor Hugo and the Marché des Carmes (see page 68), are on every morning Tues–Sun, along with the biggest (and best value) market on the Boulevard de Strasbourg (see page 98).

When it rains

In the height of Toulouse's hot summer, you'll be surprised and grateful if you get any rain. If you get a wet day the rest of the year, you won't go wrong if you take shelter in one of the city's many fantastic galleries and museums. Be aware, though, that many of them are closed on Mondays.

If it looks like the weather is setting in, head for the Cité de L'Espace (see page 90) or the Airbus site (see page 92), which is the largest aeronautical plant in Europe. The guided tours and sights, including the huge Airbus assembly hall and the first production model of Concorde, will keep adults and children amused all day.

Toulouse's many cinemas will help you stay dry in the evening. Try the Cinémathèque (see page 63) or one of the bigger multiscreen complexes in a commercial centre on the outskirts of the city. They often show English-language films in the original – check for VO, which stands for *version originale*.

When it is sunny, a great thing to do is walk round Toulouse's 50 or so *hôtel particuliers* – smart merchants' houses that date back mainly to the 15th and 16th centuries – to admire the carved exteriors. When it is raining, it's even better to head to one of these buildings that are open to visitors, such as the Hotel d'Assézat (see page 64), which houses the Fondation Bemberg. Not only does this contain a fascinating art collection, but also hosts regular events for getting children interested in art and history.

And don't forget that a spot of rain makes the perfect excuse to settle down for some serious eating. Take your pick from some of the finest restaurants in France, warm your heart and body

🔺 *The 14th-century cloister within the Musée des Augustins*

with a hearty cassoulet or other Toulouse sausage speciality, or head to the small food stands on the first floor of the Victor Hugo market to choose between dozens of good value, fresh foods.

On arrival

TIME DIFFERENCE

Toulouse is on Central European Time (GMT plus one hour). Daylight saving applies, with clocks going forward one hour in spring and back one hour in autumn on the same date as the UK.

ARRIVING
By air

Toulouse-Blagnac Airport (☎ (05) 61 42 44 00 ⓦ www.toulouse.aeroport.fr) is 8 km northwest of the centre.

The **Navette Aéroport Bus** (☎ (05) 34 60 64 00) connects to the central railway station, leaving every 20 minutes between 07.35–00.15 and returning between 05.00–20.20.

Taxis (☎ (05) 61 30 02 54) are on the Arrivals level by door C. Fares are around 22 euros for one person without luggage. The journey can take anything from 15 minutes to an hour, depending on traffic.

By rail

The main railway station is **Gare Matabiau** (ⓐ Blvd Pierre Sémard ☎ (05) 61 10 10 00). A metro station, Marengo, is directly underneath. **SNCF Train Ticket Office** ⓐ 5 rue Peyras ☎ (08) 92 35 35 35 ⓦ www.sncf.fr 🕐 09.30–18.30 Mon–Sat

By road

The central bus station, **Gare Routière** (ⓐ Blvd Pierre Sémard ☎ (05) 61 61 67 67 🕐 08.00–19.00) is right by the main railway station. A number of bus companies serve the surrounding areas.

Try **Eurolines** (☎ (05) 61 26 40 04) or **Intercars** (☎ (05) 61 58 14 53).

Traffic can be very heavy during rush hour. There are several new car parks in the centre, including at Victor Hugo, Capitole and Esquirol. For information visit ⓦ www.vincipark.com.

By water

The Canal du Midi runs right through the city centre, and you can cruise all the way to Toulouse from either Bordeaux or Marseille.

IF YOU GET LOST, TRY ...

Sorry to bother you, but...
Excusez moi de vous déranger, mais...
Ekskoozay mwah duh voo dayronjay, may...

Could you tell me the way to...
Comment fait-on pour aller a ...
Kohmohn feyt-ohn poor al-lay ah ...

Do you speak English?
Parlez-vous anglais?
Parlay vu ohnglay?

Could you point to it on my map?
Pouvez-vous me le montrer sur la carte?
Poo vay voo muh luh montray soor la kart?

FINDING YOUR FEET

If you are in Toulouse for a few days, it is worth buying a city pass, *Toulouse en Liberté*, which offers discounts on over 150 attractions around the city.

ORIENTATION

Keep the Garonne river as your main navigation point, along with the Place du Capitole. In the old part of town, most sights are within the ring of the Boulevards, in a rough square from the Botanical Gardens up to Place de Belfort in the northeast, over to the University in the northwest and then down to Place du Fer à Cheval and the Pont Saint Michel

◆ *Tree-lined avenues make the city a joy to discover on foot*

in the southwest. The Ministry of Culture offers tours of its sights and attractions. All visits last around two hours and are held daily in summer, less frequently the rest of the year. For more information contact **Arthemis** (ⓐ 6 rue Lt-Colonel Pélissier ⓣ (05) 61 12 13 14 ⓦ www.toulousevisites.com).

GETTING AROUND
Toulouse has an efficient, good value public transport system, though it's compact enough to explore on foot.

Metro, tram & train
The metro consists of five lines, A–E, although only lines A and B are classic underground lines. Line A covers 15 stations from Balma-Gramont to Basso Cambo. Line B runs from Ramonville to Borderouge, with a southern extension planned for 2013. Line C is a classic railway line with SNCF trains covering western Toulouse, connecting to line A at Arènes. Line D, another train, runs to the city of Muret. Line E is a tramway between Les Arènes metro station and Garrossos.

Bus
The local **Tisséo** bus service (ⓣ (05) 62 11 27 62 ⓦ www.tisseo.fr) runs during the day until around 20.00. There are six night buses (N1–N6) leaving from the railway station until just after midnight. La Navette is a small electric bus. Its city centre route is indicated by a dark red line on the pavement. You can hail it from anywhere along the route. Bus tickets can be bought at *tabacs* (tobacconists), newsstands, bus, tram and railway stations.

Pont de Blagnac · Route de Blagnac · Ch. de Roques · Parc Sept Deniers

B Borderouge

Bimes

Roques

Minimes - Claude Nougaro

Nougaro

Ch. Garonne

Garric Stade

Stade E. Wallon **16**

E Garrossos

Sept Deniers **16**

Soleil d'Or

Cité Madrid

Canal du Midi

1 Compans Caffarelli

Guyenne

Fourmi

Suisse

Servanty

Port de l'Embouchure

Ponts Jumeaux

Leclerc

Ancely

Ponts Jumeaux

Franklin

Barcelone Leclerc

Arenes Romaines

Loménie de Brienne

Héraciès

Purpan

Amidonniers

Colomiers Gare SNCF **C**

Casselardit

Les Abattoirs

Garonne

Saint Martin du Touch

Cartoucherie

St-Cyprien-République

12 **52** Cours Dillon

Lardenne

Le TOEC

Patte d'Oie

Zenith

C Gare St-Cyprien

Arènes

Teinturiers

Fer à Cheval

A Communicarta
Style **45** design
© Communicarta Ltd 2009 UDN.2
Map user Ref:WZFG/CS/TLS/07/0804

E

Fontaine Lestang

Rapas

Metro	Bus
A	1
B	12
C	16
D	22
E	38
	42
	52

Bénezet

Croix de Pierre

La Digue

Mermoz

Roc

38 **Empalot** Destination & Route Number

Bagatelle

Barrière de Muret

Orbesson

Mirail Université

Bernadette

Pénent

Touraine

Gallieni

A Basso Cambo

Bordelongue

12 Basso Cambo

Langlade

52 Portet H. Boucher Pinsaguel Tilleuls Roquettes Église

1 Matabiau Gare SNCF
2 Place Schuman
3 Jeanne d'Arc Bayard

(38) Amouroux
St-Jean Clinique
(42)
Balma-Gramont (A)
Argoulets
Roseraie
Église Bonnefoy
Arago
Raynal   Armagnac
Pont Matabiau
Pont Matabiau   Jolimont
Place Roquelaine
Marengo SNCF (22) (D)
A. Bernard Concorde
uportal   Riquet
Sciences Sociales (42) Jeanne d'Arc   Bachelier
Arsenal   Jean Jaurès
Capitole   (D) Murat
St-Georges   Montardy
Esquirol   François Verdier   (16)
Boulbonne   Place Dupuy   Cité de l'Hers
Aqueduc Pérignon Tilleuls
Quai de Tounis   Pont Neuf
Clinique du Château   Carmes   Place Dupuy   Port St-Etienne
Chaussée   Périsse
Salin Parlement   Grand Rond (1)   Lanfant
Jardin Royal   Belle Paule
Pont St-Michel   Leygues
Longaud   Palais de Justice   Beau Soleil
Barrau
Saint-Michel Marcel Langer   Glaïeuls
Langevin
Gers
Daste (38)   Saouzelong   Lartet
Empalot   Rangueil   (22) Gonin & Rodier
Empalot Sud   Empalot
Sainte-Agne - SNCF   Faculté de Pharmacie
Mouettes
Ramonville (B)

hour taxi stands at the railway station, at Place Wilson and at Place Esquirol. It is rather difficult to hail taxis in the street. There are also 'tourist taxis', in which drivers guide you around the main sites for around 40 euros an hour. All taxis are more expensive at night and charge extra for carrying luggage. Try **Capitole Taxi** (☎ (05) 34 25 02 50) or **Radio Taxi Toulousains** (☎ (05) 61 42 38 38).

Boat

Le Capitole (⊜ Quai de la Daurade ☎ (05) 61 11 02 33 ⏰ Mon–Sun, July–Aug; Tues–Sun, Apr–June & Oct ⓦ www.toulouse-croisieres.com Ⓜ Metro: Esquirol) is a tourist boat that sails along the Garonne river and passes historical monuments and the Île Ramier. There are night sails in summer.

For short trips on either the Garonne or Canal du Midi, try **NaviCanal** (⊜ 139 Rue Bonnat ☎ (05) 61 55 10 91 ⓦ www.navicanal.com), **Baladine** (⊜ 62 Port Saint Sauveur ☎ (05) 61 80 22 26 ⏰ Apr–Nov Ⓝ Bus: 22 to Port Saint-Etienne) or **Toulouse Croisieres** (⊜ 7 Port Saint Sauveur ☎ (05) 61 25 72 57 ⓦ www.toulouse-croisieres.com Ⓝ Bus: 22 to Port Saint-Etienne).

CAR HIRE

All major car hire firms have offices in Toulouse, mainly based at the airport and railway station. Try **Budget** (⊜ 49 rue Bayard ☎ (05) 61 63 18 18 ⓦ www.budget.com) or **Europcar** (☎ Station: (05) 62 73 41 64; airport: (08) 25 825 514 ⓦ www.europcar.com).

▶ *Hôtel Dieu Saint Jacques by the Garonne river*

THE CITY OF
Toulouse

THE CITY

The Old Town

The historic centre of Toulouse is on the Right Bank of the Garonne river, and stretches from the Grand Rond and the Palais du Justice up to the Basilique Saint Sernin. It is an attractive maze of mainly pedestrian streets packed with historic buildings and modern bars, shops and restaurants.

A good source of information on many of the monuments, churches, and events listed below is the Town Hall website ⓦ www.mairie-toulouse.fr.

SIGHTS & ATTRACTIONS

Basilique Saint Sernin

This Romanesque basilica, dating back to 1096, is one of Toulouse's most famous and most beautiful sights. Its outstanding feature is the Porte Miégeville, which opens onto the south aisle and is decorated with 12th-century sculptures. Concerts are often held here. ⓐ Pl. Saint Sernin ⓣ (05) 61 21 80 45 ⓛ 08.30–11.30, 14.00–17.30 ⓝ Metro: Capitole

The Capitole

Toulouse's 250 year old Town Hall, completed in 1759, stands proudly in the centre of the city. On the outside, eight red marble columns represent the eight 'Capitouls' of the municipality. Inside, there are frescoes and various monuments to illustrious past residents of the city. The square outside is the centre of markets and street entertainment throughout the year, and is also surrounded by lively cafés and bars. ⓐ Pl. du Capitole

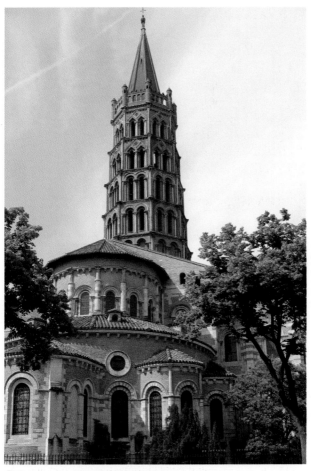

⬢ *The Romanesque basilica of Saint Sernin*

The Old Town

POI
- Ⓜ Metro Stop
- ✝ Cathedral
- ℹ Information
- ✕ Police Station
- ✈ Airport
- 🏛 Railway Stn
- ➕ Bus Station
- ➕ Hospital

BOULEVARD MONPLAISIR

ALLEE FREDERIC MISTRAL

ALLEE FREDERIC MISTRAL

Le Grand Rond

Jardin des Plantes

Halle aux Grains

Cathédrale
Paroisse
Saint-Etienne

SAINT-ETIENNE

Musée des Augustins

Musée
Paul Dupuy

RUE DU LANGUEDOC

Palais de Justice

LES CARMES

Hôtel d'Assézat
(Fondation Bemberg)

TOUNIS

Galerie de la
Halle aux Poissons

PLACE DE LA DAURADE
Église Nôtre
Dame de la
Daurade

PONT NEUF

La Garonne

Prairies
des Filtres

QUAI DE TOUNIS

AVE DE LA GARONNETTE

N

The Old Town

0   200 metres
0   200 yards

📞 (05) 61 22 51 97 🕐 09.00–19.00 Mon–Fri, 10.00–19.00 Sat
Ⓝ Metro: Capitole

Cathédrale Paroisse Saint Etienne

A brooding, immense structure that is a mix of different architectural styles, having been constructed at various times over five centuries. There are 17 chapels in here. 📍 Pl. Saint-Etienne 📞 (05) 61 51 03 82 🌐 http://cathedrale.toulouse.free.fr 🕐 08.00–19.00 Mon–Sat, 09.00–19.00 Sun Ⓝ Metro: Esquirol

Chapelle des Carmélites

In the depths of the 12th century Carmélites Convent is this beautiful small chapel, known as Toulouse's Sistine Chapel. Concerts are frequently held here. 📍 1 rue du Périgord 📞 (05) 61 21 27 60 🌐 http://carmelites.monuments-nationaux.fr 🕐 09.30–13.00, 14.00–18.00 Tues–Sun, summer; 10.00–13.00, 14.00–17.30 winter Ⓝ Metro: Capitole. Admission charge

Église Nôtre Dame de la Daurade

There are three Nôtre Dame churches in Toulouse – de la Daurade, de la Taur and de la Dalbade. This one is particularly attractive because it leads directly out onto the banks of the river. 📍 1 pl. de la Daurade 📞 (05) 61 21 38 32 🌐 www.toulouse-tourisme.com 🕐 08.30–19.00 summer; 08.30–18.30 winter Ⓝ Metro: Esquirol

Le Grand Rond & Le Jardin des Plantes (Botanical Garden)

Created during the French Revolution, this is the oldest public park in Toulouse, and over 100 different types of trees and conifers are found here. At weekends, the park gets very busy, full of families making use of the many activities, from pony trekking to roundabouts. ⓐ Allées Frederic Mistral ⓛ 07.45–dusk

Place de la Daurade

A beach in the middle of the city, right on the banks of the Garonne by the Pont Neuf bridge. Great fun during the summer. ⓜ Metro: Esquirol, then 10 min walk

CULTURE

Cinémathèque

The kind of arts cinema and exhibition space that every big city should have. Quirky film festivals held throughout the year. Great for English-language films, and a good café. ⓐ 69 rue du Taur ⓣ (05) 62 30 30 10 ⓦ www.lacinemathequedetoulouse.com ⓜ Metro: Capitole

EDF Bazacle

A strange mix of working power station and art gallery – don't think about it too much, just enjoy one of the best views of the Garonne river in the city. ⓐ 11 quai Saint Pierre ⓣ (05) 62 30 16 00 ⓦ http://fondation.edf.com ⓛ 14.00–19.00 Tues–Fri or Tues–Sun during exhibitions, Sept–July ⓜ Metro: Compans Caffarelli, then 10 min walk

Église Saint Pierre des Cuisines

The crypt under this church is the oldest building in southwest France. The church above it has been fully restored and is today a 400-seat auditorium where regular classical concerts are held.

Check with the tourist office or directly at the church for times and prices of concerts. ⓐ 12 pl. Saint Pierre ⓣ (05) 61 22 31 44 ⓦ www.toulouse.fr ⓛ 10.00–12.00, 14.00–19.00 Mon ⓝ Metro: Capitole. Admission charge

Espace Croix Baragnon

A contemporary cultural centre that is often used for large festivals in the city, such as Rio Loco (see page 10). Photography exhibitions are also regularly staged. ⓐ 24 rue Croix Baragnon ⓣ (05) 62 27 60 60 ⓦ www.toulouse.fr ⓛ 12.00–19.00 Mon–Sat ⓝ Metro: Esquirol

Galerie de la Halle aux Poissons

Tucked away down a side street next to the Garonne river and the Pont Neuf bridge, this is a funky young gallery dedicated mainly to street art and graffiti. ⓐ 11 descente de la Halle aux Poissons ⓣ (05) 61 52 67 08 ⓦ http://ghp.typepad.com ⓛ 14.00–20.00 ⓝ Metro: Capitole, then 10 min walk

Hôtel d'Assézat (Fondation Bemberg)

Very attractive former merchant's house. Its previous owner, Pierre d'Assézat, made his money in the pastel trade. Stroll into its inner courtyard to view one of the city's most well preserved 16th-century facades, or visit the private art collection inside, with many examples from the Renaissance. ⓐ Pl. d'Assézat, off rue de Metz ⓣ (05) 61 12 06 89 ⓦ www.fondation-bemberg.fr ⓛ 10.00–12.30, 13.30–18.00 Tues–Sun, open until 21.00 Thur ⓝ Metro: Esquirol. Admission charge

○ *The Hotel d'Assézat, home to the Fondation Bemberg*

Musée des Augustins

This beautiful space is worth visiting for any number of reasons – not least the exhibitions of Renaissance paintings and artefacts, with sculptures dating back to the Middle Ages. From within the museum, you can also access the Augustins Convent, a 14th century church and cloister. It is a peaceful, beautiful spot that provides a lovely break in a busy day's sightseeing. ⓐ 21 rue de Metz ⓣ (05) 61 22 21 82 ⓦ www.augustins.org ⓛ 10.00–18.00 Thur–Tues, 10.00–21.00 Wed ⓝ Metro: Esquirol. Admission charge

Musée Paul Dupuy

Museum of decorative and graphic arts. The selection is eclectic and goes right up to the present day. ⓐ 13 rue de la Pleau ⓣ (05) 61 14 65 50 ⓦ www.toulouse.fr ⓛ 10.00–18.00 Wed–Mon ⓝ Metro: Esquirol. Admission charge, students free

Musée Saint Raymond

Well located by the basilica, this houses archaeology and art from the Middle Ages. ⓐ Pl. Saint Sernin ⓣ (05) 61 22 31 44 ⓦ www.saintraymond.toulouse.fr ⓛ 10.00–18.00 Sept–May, 10.00–19.00 June–Aug ⓝ Metro: Capitole, then 10 min walk. Admission charge

Musée du Vieux Toulouse

Housed in a 16th century *hôtel particulier*, this concentrates on everyday objects that formed part of the history of the city as it developed, including old writing implements, stamps, ceramics, drinking vessels and the like. ⓐ 7 rue du May ⓣ (05) 62 27 11 50

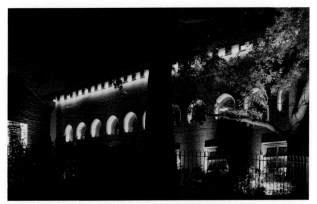

○ *Enjoy art and archaeology at the Musée Saint Raymond*

ⓦ www.toulouse-tourisme.com ⓛ 14.00–18.00 Mon–Sat, May–Oct (closed over winter) ⓝ Metro: Capitole. Admission charge

RETAIL THERAPY

The Old Town in Toulouse really is a shopper's paradise. You'll stumble across countless interesting places, from quirky vintage clothes stores to the latest chic styles from local designers on their way up to Paris couture.

Antoine et Lili Eastern-influenced clothes, and a great place to pick up beautifully packaged candles, shoes, jewellery and notebooks, all in luscious pinks, blues and yellows. ⓐ 33 rue Croix Baragnon ⓣ (05) 62 17 23 14 ⓦ www.altribu.com ⓛ 10.00–19.00 Mon–Sat ⓝ Metro: Esquirol

Diesel A large branch of this popular international boutique, and a good place to head to for stylish jeans, and unusual jackets and tops. ⓐ 4 rue Saint Antoine ⓣ (05) 61 22 82 30 ⓦ www.diesel.com ⓛ 10.00–19.30 Mon–Sat ⓜ Metro: Capitole

FNAC The best place to buy CDs, DVDs, cameras and telephones. Also has an internet café and regular photography exhibitions. ⓐ 1 pl. du Capitole ⓣ (08) 92 35 06 66 ⓦ www.fnac.com ⓛ 09.30–19.00 Mon–Fri, 20.00 Sat ⓜ Metro: Capitole

MARKETS

Besides the excellent covered Marché Victor Hugo and Marché des Carmes, open every day except Monday, there are plenty of smaller markets taking place during the week. On Tuesday and Saturday mornings, there's an organic food market in Place du Capitole. If you're looking for antiques and one-off furniture pieces, there are good markets held around the Saint Sernin basilica on Saturday and Sunday mornings, while antique book lovers should head to St Aubin on Sunday mornings. For original presents from young artists, try Place Dupuy on the first and third Friday and Saturday of every month, except August. In winter, making the most of local southwestern duck products, Place du Parlement has a foie gras market on Wednesday and Friday mornings. If you're after a good selection of local wines and knowledgeable advice, visit the wine merchant at the far end of the Marché Victor Hugo.

Hall 2 A trendy clothes shop, with a mix of international and one-off local designers. Young friendly staff. Can be expensive, but you'll walk out with something no-one else will be wearing. @ 32 rue des Marchands ☎ (05) 61 52 92 04 🕐 10.30–12.30, 14.00–19.00 Ⓜ Metro: Esquirol

Imaginarium Imaginative children's toys at this store – modern and educational, well made and with fun touches like different sized doors for children and adult shoppers. @ 40 rue de Metz ☎ (05) 61 52 50 23 Ⓦ www.imaginarium.fr 🕐 10.00–19.00 Mon–Sat Ⓜ Metro: Capitole

Nicolas The wine shop that is now spreading over much of England started out in France, and this is a particularly well stocked store. @ 6 pl. Victor Hugo ☎ (05) 61 22 18 96 Ⓦ www.nicolas.com 🕐 09.00–19.30 Mon–Sat; 10.00–13.00 Sun Ⓜ Metro: Jean-Jaurès; bus: 42

Ombres Blanches Complete heaven for book lovers. Great selection of titles, many in English, on everything from arts and poetry to travel. Wide range of contemporary and classic authors. Regular author readings. @ 50 rue Gambetta ☎ (05) 34 45 53 33 Ⓦ www.ombres-blanches.fr 🕐 10.00–19.00 Mon–Fri, 10.00–19.30 Sat Ⓜ Metro: Capitole

Violettes & Pastels Pick up some violet soaps and fragrances from this smart shop. These are classic Toulouse souvenirs. @ 10 rue St-Pantaléon ☎ (05) 61 22 14 22 Ⓦ www.violettesetpastels.fr 🕐 110.00–19.00 Tues–Sat Ⓜ Metro: Capitole

TAKING A BREAK

Toulouse is a foodie city *par excellence*. Coffee shops and salons de thé (tea shops) can be found on practically every corner, and there are an increasing number of sushi bars, tapas bars and other exotic types of cuisine.

L'Autre Salon de Thé £ ❶ Discreet café restaurant that has some of the best cakes you'll find in the city. ⓐ 45 rue des Tourneurs ⓣ (05) 61 22 11 63 ⓛ 12.00–20.00 Mon–Sat ⓜ Metro: Esquirol

Bapz £ ❷ Cheerful and popular tea house with the full range of English scones and cakes. ⓐ 13 rue de la Bourse ⓣ (05) 61 23 06 63 ⓛ 12.00–19.00 Mon–Sat ⓜ Metro: Esquirol

AFTER DARK

RESTAURANTS

Hot spots are centred around Place Saint Georges, Place President Wilson and Place du Capitole, but the countless small streets in between all hold their own treasures.

Au Père Louis £–££ ❸ A local institution that has been serving up food and drink for nearly a century. ⓐ 45 rue des Tourneurs ⓣ (05) 61 21 33 45 ⓛ 12.00–14.00, 19.00–22.30 ⓜ Metro: Esquirol

La Réserve £–££ ❹ Large windows create an airy, welcoming and modern space. Good range of pizzas and pastas. To reach it, walk down rue Ste-Ursule and turn left down rue Gambetta.

⬤ *Place Daurade in the historic Old Town*

ⓐ 8 rue Jean Suau ⓣ (05) 61 21 84 00 ⓛ 12.00–14.30, 19.00–23.00 Mon–Fri, 12.00–23.00 Sat & Sun ⓝ Bus: 54, 56; metro: Esquirol, then 10 min walk

La Braisière ££ ⑤ Right next to Place des Carmes, this lovely brasserie has red brick walls and wood beams, and cooks meat over an open fire. Terrace in summer. ⓐ 42 rue Pharaon ⓣ (05) 61 52 37 13 ⓦ www.labraisiere.fr ⓛ 11.30–14.00, 19.30–00.00 ⓝ Bus: 38, 54; metro: Esquirol, then 5 min walk

La Cave au Cassoulet ££ ⑥ Traditional, welcoming restaurant that claims to make the city's most authentic version of this famous local dish. ⓐ 54 rue Peyrolières ⓣ (05) 61 13 60 30

🕐 19.00–22.00 Wed & Thur, 12.00–14.00, 19.00–22.00 Fri–Mon
🚍 Bus: 54, 56; metro: Esquirol, then 10 min walk

Les Caves de la Marechale ££ ❼ The best thing to do in
this atmospheric old vaulted cellar is give yourself over
to the chef's suggestions. Live music on the last Friday of
every month. 🅐 3 rue Jules Chalande ☎ (05) 61 23 89 88
🌐 www.lescavesdelamarechale.com 🕐 12.00–14.00,
20.00–22.00 Tues–Fri & Sun, 20.00–00.00 Sat 🚇 Metro:
Capitole, Esquirol

Brasserie des Beaux-Arts ££–£££ ❽ Next to the Pont Neuf
bridge, this is the place to come for seafood platters and to
watch locals enjoy their evening aperitif. 🅐 1 Quai de la Daurade
☎ (05) 61 21 12 12 🕐 12.00–14.30, 19.00–23.00 🚍 Bus: 54, 56;
metro: Esquirol, then 10 min walk

Jardins de l'Opéra £££ ❾ Chef Stephen Tournie has
made this restaurant one of the most sought after (and
expensive) in the city. 🅐 1 pl. du Capitole ☎ (05) 61 23 07 76
🌐 www.lesjardinsdelopera.com 🕐 12.00–14.00, 20.00–22.00,
Tues–Sat 🚇 Metro: Capitole

BARS & CLUBS

If you're up for a good time, Toulouse can provide it. This is just
a small selection of the many bars, clubs and cafés that go on
long into the night. Most don't even start filling up until 23.00,
so don't set your alarm clock too early.

La Cale Sèche Crowded, smoky, fun bar just off Place du Capitole, specialising in all types of lethal rums. Inside it is dark and dingy, with lots of exposed wood beams and a long wooden bar. ⓐ 41 rue Gambetta ⏱ 19.30–01.30 Mon & Tues, 13.00–01.30 Wed–Sat Ⓝ Metro: Capitole

Le Glou Glou Cafe Live music is on most nights at this Caribbean-style bar – get into the spirit of things with a few rum cocktails. ⓐ 4 rue Victor Hugo ☎ (05) 61 21 80 92 ⏱ 11.00–02.00 Ⓝ Metro: Jean-Jaurès

Le Mandala Jazz club with weekly live music shows. In summer, there's a terrace here that is perfect for chilling out with a long cold drink. ⓐ 23 rue des Amidonniers. ☎ (05) 6121 10 05 ⓦ www.lemandala.com ⏱ 21.00–late, depending on programme Ⓝ Bus: 1

L'Opus A lively DJ bar where the good times go on until late. ⓐ 24 rue Bachelier ☎ (05) 61 62 37 46 ⏱ 20.00–01.00 Ⓝ Metro: Jean-Jaurès

Senso Popular with the thirty-something crowd, this sleek bar not far from Place President Wilson is open until dawn. ⓐ 6 rue Bayard ⏱ 20.00–late Ⓝ Metro: Jean-Jaurès

Le Velane Baroque-style bar and brasserie with lively jazz music most weekends. ⓐ 3 pl. Montoulieu, Grand Rond ☎ (05) 61 53 60 56 ⓦ www.levelane.com ⏱ 12.00–14.30, 18.30–01.00 Ⓝ Metro: St-Cyprien-République

THE CITY

Île Ramier & the Left Bank

The Garonne divides near Saint-Michel bridge, creating the two branches that embrace Ramier Island. In the middle are three huge complexes: the Parc des Expositions, the Stadium and Ramier Park. The two branches of the river come together again near Empalot, close to the Science Faculties and Pech-David hill. On the far side stretches the Left Bank, with its rising property values and increasingly chic *quartiers* (districts). The Left Bank is the bohemian artists' corner, centred around a fantastic museum of modern art, and with a number of other interesting bars and galleries. Saint Cyprien is a particularly lively, up-and-coming area.

◆ *View of the Dome de la Grave through the Pont des Catalans*

74

SIGHTS & ATTRACTIONS

Chapelle St Christophe
Small Catholic chapel with some intricate carvings on its interior and exterior walls. ⓐ Av. Lamartine Ⓝ Metro: Fontaine-Lestang

Dôme de la Grave
Part of another working hospital complex, the striking feature for visitors here is a large 18th-century copper dome that contains a circular chapel. You can only admire it from the outside, but it's a lovely stroll through the four attractive inner courtyards and pretty gardens to get there. ⓐ Pl. Lange ⓣ (05) 61 77 78 33 ⓛ Gardens: 08.00–20.00 Ⓝ Metro: St-Cyprien-République

Hippodrome de la Cepière
Horse racing and casino. The course and surrounding greenery

POI
Metro Stop
Cathedral
Information
Police Station
Airport
Railway Stn
Bus Station
Hospital

Le Zenith

CEPIERE-POLYGONE

Arènes

Hippodrome
de la
Cepière

Chapelle
St Christope

Mermoz

Fontaine
Lestang

Parc Fontaine
Lestang

**Île Ramier &
the Left Bank**

0   200 metres
0   200 yards

La Garonne

Théâtre
Garonne

Bazacle

Église Saint Pierre
des Cuisines

PLACE
SAINT-PIERRE

QUAI ST-PIERRE

RUE VALADE

RUE PARGAMINIERS

RUE DE BOURRASSOL

AVE DU CHÂTEAU D'EAU

ALLÉE ALLÉE CHARLE MALPEL

RUE DES FONTAINES

Les Abattoirs

Dôme de la
Grave

Jardin
Raymond VI

Centre Municipal de
l'Affiche, de la Carte
Postale de l'Art Graphique

PLACE DU
RAVELIN

PONT DES CATALANS

CHARLES

RUE VILLENEUVE

PLACE
LANGE

PONT ST-PIERRE

QUAI S.T LOMBARD

LA BOURSE

RUE DES BLANCHERS

RUE MALBEC

PLACE DE
LA DAURADE

RUE PEYROLIERES

RUE CUJAS

Hôtel Dieu
Saint Jacques
(Musée de la
Médicine)

Église Nôtre
Dame de la
Daurade

RUE DE METZ

R DJUR ROUX

R DJUR BRUN

RUE DES CONSULS

RUE ADOLPHE COLL

PLACE DU
RAVELIN

R GANELY

St-Cyprien
République

GRANDE RUE ST-NICOLAS

PONT NEUF

D124

Galerie de la
Halle aux Poissons

RUE DES
COUTELIERS

PATTE D'OIE

RUE DE L'ABREUVOIR

M Patte d'Oie

RUE DU TCHAD

N124

AVE ETIENNE BILLIERS

St Cyprien
Market

PLACE
ROGUET

RUE DE GASCOGNE

RUE DE FENOUILLET

RUE CADACHE

RUE DE CUGNAUX

MJC Roguet

M

RUE DE LANCRY

RUE DE VARSOVIE

Espace
Saint-Cyprien

RUE DE LA REPUBLIQUE

RUE CHARBONNEL

RUE DES TEINTURIERS

RUE DE CYPRIEN

RUE DES TEINTURIERS

Galerie du
Château d'Eau

TOUNIS

Prairie
des Filtres

DE

FITTE

COURS DILLON

RUE LAGANNE

AVE DE LA GARONNETTE

QUAI DE TOUNIS

SAINT-CYPRIEN

RUE DE CHIRIBOU

RUE LEBRE

RUE CLÉMENT

RUE STE LUCIE

RUE H
CAMPAGNO

RUE H
LAVIGNE

RUE CANY

RUE FINES
ST-CYPRIEN

PLACE DU
FER À CHEVAL

PONT SAINT MICHEL

N133

Île Ramier

La Garonne

CHEMIN DE LA NÉBOULE

RUE DES ARCS SAINT-CYPRIEN

R A VALAYS

RUE DE CLAIRFONT

CIMETIÈRE

RUE DRAINES

RUE GASTON PHOEBUS

RUE RAPAS

RUE BENEZKY

Lycée Déodat
de Séverac

AVE

DE

MURET

Institut Universitaire
de Formation des Maîtres

DE SÉVERAC

AVE A MASSONNIE

Parc des
Expositions

ALLÉE JOURDAIN

ROND POINT
MICHEL
BENECH

Stadium
Municipal
de Toulouse
& Parc du Ramier

AVE DU GRAND RAMIER

PORT GIRAUD

BOULEVARD DU MARECHAL JUIN

RUE DES PLATANES

RUE HENRI TACHÈRES

The Summer Pool

cover 34 hectares and there are 53 race meetings per year.
ⓐ 1 chemin des Courses ☎ (05) 61 49 27 24 ⓦ www.hippodrome-toulouse.com Ⓝ Metro: Patte-d'Oie

Hôtel Dieu Saint Jacques

Built in the 12th century, this was originally a stop for pilgrims along the Route de Saint Jacques de Compostelle before becoming Toulouse's first large hospital. Today, some of it is still an active hospital, while other parts are open for exploring, including the lovely gardens, and a first floor balcony with views of the river. ⓐ 2 rue Viguerie ☎ (05) 61 77 82 33 🕐 Public areas open most days Ⓝ Metro: St-Cyprien-République

Jardin Raymond VI

Right on the banks of the Garonne, behind Les Abattoirs modern art museum (see opposite), this is one of the liveliest city parks. Every weekend it is full of families enjoying the large children's play area, and spilling out from the gallery to enjoy the view of the river as water cascades over the weir. Good jogging and cycling paths along the river at this point also. ⓐ 76 allée Charles-de-Fitte Ⓝ Bus: 1; metro: St-Cyprien-République, then 10 min walk

Parc des Expositions (Exhibition Centre)

Regular events from antiques fairs to sports meetings are held at this large exhibition centre on the Île Ramier. ⓐ Rond Point Michel Benech ☎ (05) 62 25 45 45 ⓦ www.toulouseexpo.fr
Ⓝ Bus: 12, 52 (Left Bank); metro: Les Arènes then Bus: 31

Parc Fontaine Lestang

Small but well maintained park in an increasingly chic neighbourhood. ⓐ Rue Fieux ⓛ 07.45–dusk ⓝ Metro: Mermoz

Prairie des Filtres

Large green park along the banks of the Garonne. It gets busy at lunchtime with picnicking locals. Sporting events, festivals, concerts and firework displays are often held here. ⓐ Cours Dillon ⓝ Metro: St-Cyprien-République

Parc du Ramier

This recreation ground is part of the exhibition centre and stadium complex, and is often full of city sports team and amateur rugby players practising on weekend mornings. It stretches along the length of the island. ⓐ Île Ramier ⓛ 07.00–dusk ⓝ Bus: 12, 52 (Left Bank)

CULTURE

Les Abattoirs

Since its opening in 2000, this has become one of France's most exciting contemporary art museums. Housed in a disused 19th century abattoir, its cavernous rooms contain a mass of sculptures, installations and works of art. The collection comprises over 2000 works, including painting, sculpture, mixed media and multimedia by artists from 44 countries. ⓐ 76 allée Charles-de-Fitte ⓣ (05) 62 48 58 00 ⓦ www.lesabattoirs.org ⓛ 12.00–20.00 Tues–Sun, summer; 11.00–19.00 Tues–Sun, winter ⓝ Metro: St-Cyprien-République; bus: 1. Admission charge

○ *The striking Les Abattoirs museum of modern art*

Centre Municipal de l'Affiche, de la Carte Postale et de l'Art Graphique

An art centre for posters, postcards and graphic arts that not only sells a number of excellent cards but also has a large collection of illustrations from comic books and more traditional artistic outlets. The building also contains a library, video library and workshops. ⓐ 58 allée Charles-de-Fitte ⓣ (05) 61 59 24 64 ⓦ www.centreaffiche.toulouse.fr ⓛ 09.00–12.00, 14.00–18.00 Mon–Fri ⓜ Metro: St-Cyprien-République; bus: 1

Espace Saint-Cyprien

Large contemporary arts space with music, theatre, the Chapeau Rouge bar and an art gallery of photography and

sculpture. 📍 56 allée Charles-de-Fitte 📞 (05) 61 22 27 77
🕐 09.00–12.30, 13.30–18.30 Mon–Fri, 9.30–12.00 Sat 🅼 Metro:
Saint-Cyprien-République; bus: 1, 3, 14

Galerie du Château d'Eau

One of Toulouse's most unusual and rewarding galleries, this
contemporary photographer's gallery is housed in a water
tower. The exhibitions change frequently, and often deal with
a specific theme such as alienation or global warming, with
numerous different photographers giving their take on a single
issue. 📍 1 pl. Laganne, just across Pont Neuf 📞 (05) 61 77 09 40
🆆 www.galeriechateaudeau.org 🕐 13.00–19.00 Tues–Sun
🅼 Metro: St-Cyprien-République. Admission charge, under
18s free

M J C Roguet

Exhibition space with ever-evolving range of contemporary
artists, mainly sculpture and projected imagery. 📍 9 rue de
Gascogne 📞 (05) 61 77 26 00 🕐 9.30–12.30, 14.00–19.00 Tues–Fri;
14.00–19.00 Sat & Mon 🆆 www.mjcroguet.com 🅼 Metro:
Patte-d'Oie

Musée de la Médecine

Interesting and unusual museum looking specifically at medical
development in Toulouse. You'll find a collection of gruesome
medical instruments as well as sculptures and paintings.
📍 Hôtel Dieu Saint Jacques, 2 rue Viguerie 📞 (05) 61 77 84 25
🆆 http://museemedecine.free.fr 🕐 11.00–17.00 Thur–Sat
🅼 Metro: St-Cyprien-République

Théâtre Garonne

This 250-seat theatre provides a stage for many visiting theatre groups and contemporary productions. 1 av. du Château d'Eau (05) 62 48 54 77 www.theatregaronne.com Metro: St-Cyprien-République

RETAIL THERAPY

It can take some digging around to find the best shops over on this side of the river, but it is fantastic for bargains, more unusual food stuffs and creations by young artists and designers. There is a collection of interesting regional and exotic food shops, and new boutiques are springing up all the time – a clear sign of how dynamic this area has become. The best market is held in Saint Cyprien, but you'll often find the smaller squares attract a smattering of local stalls selling photographs, organic produce or music.

Marché Saint Cyprien A picturesque and popular market, held every morning except Mondays. A wide range of local food producers set up their stalls within the original *halle* (market hall). Pl. Roguet 07.00–13.00 Metro: St-Cyprien-République

Place de la Patte d'Oie This area was originally called Reine Pédauque, after a Roman aqueduct that used to exist here. In the Occitan language, *pédauque* became *patte d'oie*. Today it is a bustling intersection of three major roads, and the site of some good shops. Metro: Patte-d'Oie

Saint Cyprien & Patte-d'Oie Bustling local neighbourhood with everything from pet stores to delicatessens to small clothing boutiques. A great place for finding exotic ingredients for Thai or Indian curries. Historically, this area was subject to frequent flooding, and as such attracted the poor, sick or immigrant communities that the more affluent parts of town rejected. All that has changed, and with the arrival of the metro house prices have been rocketing and the excellent shops have been moving in. The main shops are centred around Rue de la République and Place de la Patte d'Oie. ⊙ Metro: Patte-d'Oie

⊙ *Deliciously nutty nougat from Toulouse*

TAKING A BREAK

Increasingly trendy bars and restaurants are centred
around Place Saint Cyprien, Place de la Patte d'Oie and
Rue de la République.

Bar le Ravelin £ ❶ Open from very early until very late, making
this bustling, friendly and a great meeting place. Piano music
and tapas some evenings. ⓐ 6 pl. du Ravelin ❶ (05) 61 42 93 32
🕐 07.00–02.00 Ⓜ Metro: St-Cyprien-République

Le Bistrot des Halles Saint Cyprien £–££ ❷ Friendly and
popular café bar and bistro with good food at excellent
prices. ⓐ 17 pl. Roguet ❶ (05) 62 48 93 86 🕐 07.00–00.00
Ⓜ Metro: Patte-d'Oie

L'Hemicycle £–££ ❸ Restaurant, café and salon de thé in
the gardens of Les Abattoirs, a great place to come even if
you're not visiting the gallery. ⓐ 76 allée Charles-de-Fitte
❶ (05) 62 87 73 06 🕐 11.00–14.30 Tues, 11.00–22.00 Wed & Thur,
11.00–23.00 Fri & Sat, 11.00–19.00 Sun Ⓜ Metro: St-Cyprien-
République; bus: 1

AFTER DARK

RESTAURANTS
Ecuries d'Athena ££ ❹ Local specialities including a very good
cassoulet. Some vegetarian options also. Small terrace garden
at the back. Good wine list of over 400 bottles, and you can

go into the cellar and pick your own bottle. 🅐 65 allée Charles-de-Fitte 🅣 (05) 61 59 77 11 🅦 www.ecuriesathena.com
🅛 12.00–14.00, 19.30–22.00 Mon–Fri, 19.30–22.00 Sat
🅝 Metro: St-Cyprien-République

BARS & CLUBS

Le Chapeau Rouge Concerts and DJ nights are held most weeks at this hip venue. 🅐 56 allée Charles-de-Fitte 🅣 (05) 61 22 27 77 🅛 Enquire for concert dates 🅝 Metro: St-Cyprien-République

Hall 7, Parc Expo International DJs regularly play in this cavernous space, perfect for massive club nights. 🅐 Île du Ramier 🅣 08 92 68 36 22 / 08 92 39 01 00 🅛 22.00 til late, on club nights (always check ahead) 🅝 Bus: 12, 52 (Left Bank)

Le Kléo/Le Ramier Club nights with experimental DJs, from punk and disco to house. 🅐 1 av. du Grand Ramier, Île du Ramier 🅣 (05) 61 52 86 63 🅛 22.00–late on club nights (always check ahead) 🅝 Bus: 12, 52 (Left Bank)

Le Zénith The biggest stadium in France, with seating for 9,000 people. Its size and glamorous architecture means it has no problem attracting big international names. Club nights are also held here regularly. 🅐 11 av. Raymond Badiou 🅣 (05) 62 74 49 49 🅛 Times vary, always check ahead 🅝 Metro: Patte-d'Oie or Arénes

The Boulevards & further afield

Outside of the Old City, there is still plenty to see. The Boulevards that ring Toulouse follow the course of the canal, and have various access points on to the tow path. And as you get further out from downtown you'll experience the change from traditional to high tech Toulouse, as the aeronautical and space industries are based out here.

SIGHTS & ATTRACTIONS

Aerothèque

A comprehensive exhibition of the history of aeronautics in Toulouse. ⓐ 18 rue Montmorency ⓣ (05) 61 93 93 57 ⓦ www.aerotheque.fr ⓛ 14.00–17.00 Wed; other weekdays by appointment ⓝ Bus: 15 to Compans Caffarelli gardens. Admission charge

Les Ailes Anciennes

This is where old airplanes go to die, or rather to be gazed at by enthusiastic plane spotters. Booking is compulsory. ⓐ Av. Edouard Serres, Colomiers ⓣ (05) 61 21 70 01 ⓦ www.aatlse.org ⓛ Guided tours 09.30 and 10.30 Sat ⓝ Train: Colomiers Gare. Admission charge

Amphithéâtre Romain de Purpan

Built around the first century, one of the best ways to explore this well preserved amphitheatre is by guided tour on a Sunday. Booking is required. Gladiator conquests were held here until

🔺 *Aeronautical and high-tech Toulouse*

the end of the fourth century and the tour gives you plenty of gruesome stories. ⓐ Av. des Arènes Romaines ⓣ (05) 61 22 31 44 ⓦ www.arena-stadium.eu.org ⓛ 14.00–18.00 Sun, June & Sept; 14.00–19.00 Sun; July–Aug ⓝ Bus: 66 to Cauterets, 70 to rue de Purpan. Admission charge

Arnaud-Bernard
Pretty part of town near Jardin Compans Caffarelli, with some interesting shops to explore. To the west, wander into Saint Pierre and Amidonniers, and down to the Garonne river.

Canal du Midi
See feature on page 16.

ongrès Pierre Baudis

lass and stainless steel building, an interesting
stop on a walking tour of the city. It is not open for general
visits. ⓐ 11 Esplanade Compans Caffarelli ⓣ (05) 62 30 40 40
ⓦ www.centre-congres-toulouse.fr ⓝ Bus: 15, 70, 71

Cité de L'Espace

Toulouse's space park, where you look round a replica of the MIR
space station, watch movies at the IMAX theatre, play games and
visit a more serious exhibition showcasing how satellite phones
work. See what is just around the corner for the communication
industry. For younger children, there's an excellent Young
Astronauts play area, where the slide comes out of a huge play
rocket. ⓐ Parc de la Plaine, av. Jean Gonord ⓣ (05) 62 71 48 71
ⓦ www.cite-espace.com ⓛ 09.00–18.00 Mon–Fri, 09.00–19.00
Sat & Sun ⓝ Bus: 19, 35; metro: Marengo then Bus: 31. Admission
charge

Église Saint Aubin

A handsome Catholic church dating from the 13th century, standing
in the middle of a very pleasant large square. Every Sunday there's
a good market in this increasingly sought-after neighbourhood.
ⓐ Pl. St Aubin, off blvd Michelet ⓣ (05) 61 62 64 21
ⓦ http://catholique-toulouse.cef.fr ⓛ Services: 10.00 Sun
ⓝ Metro: Jean-Jaurès, then walk along rue de la Comobette
towards Boulevard Riquet

Église Saint Nicolas de la Grave

Large Orthodox church with an attractive façade and

THE BOULEVARDS & FURTHER A

lovely stained glass inside. ⓐ 302 av. de Grande-Bretagne
ⓣ (05) 61 31 92 25 ⓦ www.toulouse.fr ⓛ Services: 17.30 Sat
ⓜ Metro: Patte d'Oie plus a 10 min walk

Jardin Compans Caffarelli

Ten hectares of park, with a Japanese garden that gives access
to the Canal du Midi. The artificial hills, raked gravel geometric
designs, wooden bridge and teahouse all create a magical
atmosphere. At the far end of the park there's a large lake,
which has a children's playground and a refreshments kiosk.
ⓐ Blvd Lascrosses ⓛ 07.45–18.00 ⓜ Bus: 15, 70, 71

Jolimont Observatoire

The observatory was built in 1846 and today, although no

THE 'GREEN LUNGS' OF TOULOUSE

Bookmarking the city to the north, south, east and west
are four large green spaces, collectively known as the
city's *zones vertes* (green spaces). They make relaxing days
or afternoons out, and are good for dog walking, picnics
or jogging. Les Argoulets, to the east, has 45 hectares of
rugby and baseball pitches with judo space and an ice rink.
Pech-David, to the south, is a 270 hectare park overlooking
the Garonne river. La Ramée, to the west, is 280 hectares
and has a large fishing lake, sailing lake and archery range.
Sesquières, to the north, is a 117 hectare park with water
skiing on the lake in summer time.

...ed, is open to visitors and school groups. It has lovely,
... ...own gardens all around, and is rather ramshackle,
but it is great fun for children. The view from the dome on
Friday nights can be breathtaking. **a** 1 av. Camille Flammarion,
off av. de la Colonne into allée des Acacias **t** (05) 61 58 42 01
w www.imcce.fr **L** Gardens: 07.45–18.00; Observatory Dome:
21.00 Fri for a free tour **N** Metro: Jolimont

La Péniche Maison de la Violette (Violet House Barge)

An unusual experience can be had on board the Violet House
Barge. Violets, in flower from November to March, have been
grown in Toulouse for 150 years. This permanently moored
barge is part museum, part shop devoted entirely to the
flowers. It sells a range of all things violet – from honey to
marmalade, tea, perfumes and shower gels. **a** Blvd de Bonrepos
t (05) 61 99 01 30 **w** www.lamaisondelaviolette.fr **L** 14.00–19.00
Mon, 10.00–12.30, 14.00–19.00 Tues–Sat (closed second week of
January) **N** Metro: Marengo; bus: 15, 16, 22, 21, 41

Site Airbus & Clement Adler

The largest aeronautical site in Europe is open to visitors
for guided tours by prior appointment only. You can tour
both the double decker Airbus and a model of the original
Concorde. Booking is compulsory. **a** 10 av. Guynemer, Colomiers
t (05) 61 18 06 01 **w** www.taxiway.fr **L** Mon–Fri by appointment
N Train to Colomiers Gare. Admission charge

O *The aeronautical industry has boosted the city's growth*

Touch and Go

Find out what goes on behind the scenes of an airport, from checking in bags to retrieving lost luggage. Guided tours for groups only. Booking is compulsory. 🅐 Aérogare Aviation d'Affaires, Blagnac 🆃 (05) 61 71 62 11 🆆 http://touchandgo.free.fr 🅻 Mon–Sat by appointment 🅝 Bus: Navette Aéroport, 17, 66. Admission charge

CULTURE

Archives Municipales

Documentation centre that contains some interesting old photos of the city. There are also good historical picture books for sale in the shop. 🅐 2 rue des Archives 🆃 (05) 61 61 63 33 🆆 www.archives.mairie-toulouse.fr 🅻 09.00–17.00 Mon–Fri 🅝 Metro: Roseraie

Café Théâtre Les Minimes

Theatre and bar with a range of excellent smaller productions. Well worth the trip out to the far side of the Boulevards, north of the centre. 🅐 6 rue Gélibert 🆃 (05) 62 72 06 36 🆆 www.lesminimes.com 🅻 Shows: 21.00 Wed–Sat; times vary so call ahead 🅝 Bus: 10. Admission charge for shows

Halle aux Grains

Hexagonal concert hall and exhibition space that sees a lively contemporary arts programme throughout the year, from visiting pianists to operas. The Orchestre du Capitole has its base here. The building itself was a covered market used for trading cereals

from 1864 until 1952, when it became a sports centre. It was
finally converted into a concert hall in 1974. 🅰 Pl. Dupuy 🅣 (05)
61 63 13 13 🅦 www.onct.mairie-toulouse.fr 🅛 Opening hours
vary, depending on programme. Call ahead for details. 🅝 Bus: 16;
metro: Jean-Jaurès, then 10 min walk

Instituto Cervantes

A cultural space dedicated to Spanish and Basque culture.
Almost all exhibitions are presented in both Spanish and
French. 🅰 31 rue des Chalets, off blvd d'Arcole 🅣 (05) 61 62 48 64
🅦 http://toulouse.cervantes.es 🅛 10.00–15.00 Mon–Fri,
Sept–July 🅝 Bus: 61, 42

Le Médiathèque José Cabanis

A strikingly modern building, and a welcome piece of architecture
amid the sprawl of Toulouse's outer boulevards. It contains
an arts centre, a media library named after José Cabanis
(a writer from Toulouse who died in 2000), and hosts
a wide range of cultural and leisure activities for adults and
teenagers. There are some early learning activities for children.
You will also find a fantastic documentary collection in every
possible format, from books to CDs, videos, DVDs and online.
🅰 1 allée Jacques Chaban-Delmas 🅣 (05) 62 27 40 00
🅛 10.00–19.00 Tues, Wed, Fri & Sat; 14.00–19.00 Thurs;
14.00–18.00 Sun 🅦 www.bibliothequedetoulouse.fr 🅝 Metro:
Marengo. Admission charge, under 18s free

Musée Georges Labit

Unusual works of art at this intimate museum, concentrating

🔺 *Oriental and Egyptian art at Musée Georges Labit*

almost entirely on Asia and Ancient Egypt. ⓐ 17 rue du Japon
ⓣ (05) 61 14 65 50 ⓦ www.toulouse-tourisme.com ⓛ 10.00–17.00
Wed–Mon ⓝ Bus: 78, 79, 80. Admission charge

Musée de la Résistance et de la Déportation

Part museum, part memorial, part research centre, this collection
is centred around Toulouse and southwest France during World
War II. Expect plenty of honest exhibits about collaboration as
well as the resistance movement. ⓐ 52 allée des Demoiselles
ⓣ (05) 61 14 80 40 ⓦ www.musee-resistance31.fr ⓛ 09.30–12.00,
14.00–18.00 Mon–Fri, 14.00–17.00 Sat ⓝ Bus: 10, 78, 79, 80

THE BOULEVARDS & FURTHER AF

RETAIL THERAPY

Once you get out to the Boulevards and beyond, a lot of the best shopping is centred around the commercial centres. Although less romantic than downtown, parking is easy and many of the best shops are located in one space.

La Cave Spirituelle Wine shop with wide choice of regional bottles and exceptionally helpful staff. Delivery available also – free locally for orders above 75 euros. ⓐ 21 pl. Arnaud Bernard ❶ (05) 61 22 64 55 ⓦ www.wines-and-spirits.com ❷ 10.00–12.30, 15.00–19.30 Mon–Sat Ⓝ Metro: Jeanne d'Arc or Compans Caffarelli

Centre Commercial Compans Large centre with a variety of clothes and interior shops, plus a FNAC for concert tickets (see page 20). ⓐ 3 esplanade Compans Caffarelli ❷ 08.00–20.00 Mon–Sat Ⓝ Bus: 60, 61, 69; metro: Compans Caffarelli

Centre Commercial Carrefour, Portet-sur-Garonne The largest in Toulouse, with a wide variety of international and local shops. ⓐ Blvd de l'Europe, Portet-sur-Garonne ❶ (05) 61 72 10 51 Ⓝ Bus: 47 from Basso Combo

Cultura Music, books and technology at this well stocked store. ⓐ 12 blvd de l'Europe (opposite Carrefour), Portet-sur-Garonne ❶ (05) 61 72 39 48 ⓦ www.cultura.com Ⓝ Bus: 47 from Basso Combo

Imaginarium A large branch of this fantastic children's store, with modern educational games and toys. ⓐ Centre Commercial Carrefour,

…Garonne ☎ (05) 62 20 25 84 Ⓦ www.imaginarium.fr
🕐 10.00–19.00 Mon–Sat Ⓝ Bus: 47, 49 to Portet Gare

Marché du Boulevard de Strasbourg Lively market selling fruit,
vegetables and a wide variety of foodstuffs. ⓐ Blvd de Strasbourg
🕐 07.00–11.00 Ⓝ Metro: Jean-Jaurès

TAKING A BREAK

L'Art de Vivre £ ❶ Five minutes from the airport at Blagnac,
this is a sophisticated, welcoming restaurant with an attractive
leafy terrace. ⓐ 279 chemin Ramelet Moundi, Tournefeuille
☎ (05) 61 07 52 52 Ⓦ www.lartdevivre.fr 🕐 12.00–14.00, 19.30–22.00
Thur–Sat, 12.00–14.00 Sun–Tues Ⓝ Bus: 63, 21 to Tournefeuille

L'Entrecôte £ ❷ There's no menu here, and if you don't like steak
and frites, you're best off going elsewhere. For meat lovers it's an
excellent choice and consequently popular; get there early or
be prepared to queue. ⓐ 15 blvd de Strasbourg ☎ (05) 61 21 87 18
Ⓦ www.entrecote.fr 🕐 12.00–14.00, 19.15–22.45 Ⓝ Metro: Jean-Jaurès

AFTER DARK

RESTAURANTS
Boca Chica ££ ❸ The large terrace on the shores of Sesquières
lake is used to maximum effect at this beach-themed restaurant.
Cheesy but fun. ⓐ Lac de Sesquières, allée des Foulques
☎ (05) 61 70 37 70 Ⓦ www.bocachica.fr 🕐 19.00–02.00
Wed–Sat Ⓝ Best to take a taxi

◯ *Narrow streets mean some creative parking in the Old Town*

L'Amphitryon ££–£££ ❹ Upscale restaurant where chef Yannick Delpech conjures up creations that are definitely worth the trip. ⓐ Chemin de Gramont, Colomiers ⓣ (05) 61 15 55 55 ⓦ www.lamphitryon.com ⓛ 12.00–14.30, 19.30–23.00 ⓝ Metro: Jolimont, then 15 min walk

Michel Sarran ££–£££ ❺ Good value for a gastronomic, Michelin-starred restaurant. Book ahead. ⓐ 21 blvd Armand Duporta, off blvd Lascrosses ⓣ (05) 61 12 32 32 ⓦ www.michel-sarran.com ⓛ 12.00–13.45, 20.00–21.45 Mon, Tues, Thur & Fri, 20.00–21.45 Wed ⓝ Bus: 25

BARS & CLUBS
Le Purple Currently one of the coolest night spots in the city. ⓐ 2 rue Castellane ⓣ (05) 62 73 04 67 ⓦ www.le-purple.com ⓛ 22.00–05.00 Tues–Sat ⓝ Metro: Jean-Jaurès

Rest'ô Jazz Lively and charming night spot, with live music and well priced, generous food. ⓐ 8 rue Amélie ⓣ (05) 61 57 96 95 ⓦ www.restojazz.com ⓛ 20.00–02.00 Mon–Sat ⓝ Metro: Marengo

Casino Salies-du-Salat Large modern casino complex, with restaurants and slot machines. ⓐ Blvd de Casino, Salies du Salat ⓣ (05) 61 33 37 77 ⓦ www.omnium-casinos.com ⓛ 10.00–04.00 Mon–Fri, 10.00–05.00 Sat & Sun ⓝ Bus: free bus from Matabiau. Admission charge

---

❶ *The road to Albi in the Pyrénées*

OUT OF TOWN
trips

The Pyrénées

One of the great things about Toulouse is how close it is to the mountains of the Pyrénées. This means walking, mountain biking and canoeing in summer, and skiing in winter. There are also a number of thermal spa resorts, and plenty of local crafts and dishes to enjoy. As you get closer to the Spanish border, both the dialect and the dishes take on a more southern Mediterranean feeling, and the ability to dip in and out of both countries also makes for a fascinating trip.

GETTING THERE

The Pyrénées is a huge area, covering 430 km from the Mediterranean to the Atlantic and forming a natural barrier between France and Spain. It is roughly split into three sections – the Pyrénées Atlantiques by Biarritz and the Basque country, the Hautes Pyrénées, and the Pyrénées Orientales towards Roussillon and the Côte d'Azur. From Toulouse, the easiest and quickest section to get to is the Hautes Pyrénées. You can be within its foothills in about an hour from Toulouse, although with a few more days, a lot more is possible.

By rail
There are many trains that go from Toulouse central railway station to the Haute Garonne and Pyrénées. The most interesting is **Le Train Jaune** (the Yellow Train ⓦ www.trainstouristiques-ter.com/train_jaune.htm), which travels through the Tet valley high into the Pyrénées, then descends into Spain and ends up in Barcelona.

🔺 *Foix's castle dominates the surrounding countryside*

Since 2005, the train itself – although still yellow –
has been modernised.

SNCF timetable and bookings Ⓦ www.sncf.com

By road

Heading out of Toulouse by car, take the A66. The N20 road then
leads you through the Haut Garonne to Foix, the best starting
point for the Ariège valley. For Andorra, continue on the N20
through Tarascon-sur-Ariège and Aix-les-Thermes, then take
the tiny N2 that winds up through increasingly steep scenery.
Alternatively, for the Atlantic side of the mountain range, take
the A64 from Toulouse, which leads over to Bayonne and Lourdes.

Around Toulouse

| | 0 | 25 km |
| | 0 | 15 miles |

Key:
- City
- Large Town
- Small Town
- POI
- Motorway
- Main Road
- Minor Road
- Airport
- Railway

OUT OF TOWN

Tour buses travelling from Toulouse throughout the region depart from the central bus station (see page 48) and from **Courriers de la Garonne** (ⓐ 133 chemin du Sang de Serp ⓣ (05) 62 72 37 23 ⓦ www.courriersdelagaronne.com).

SIGHTS & ATTRACTIONS

Andorra

The independent principality of Andorra is only 90 minutes from Toulouse and is a duty-free haven, so it makes a good

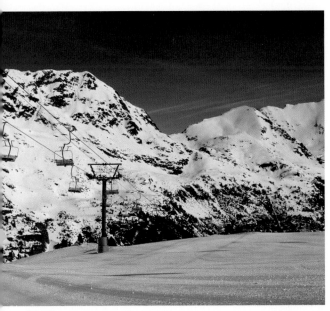

⬥ *Andorra – a beginner skier's paradise*

day trip to stock up on perfumes and wines or spirits. It is also a base for skiing, with several family-friendly resorts on either side, and there are a number of good restaurants and bars. Since EU borders have become open, border checks by the *douanes volantes* (free-ranging customs officers) have become less frequent. But be aware, as customs officials can stop you for a routine check anywhere they like. Because of the tax-free status of Andorra, checks are regular on the N20 road.

SKIING

Skiing in the Pyrénées is lower than in the Alps and the slopes are often easier, perfect for beginners and for families. Snowboarding is popular. The first slopes start just over an hour from Toulouse, but the higher you go, the better they are. A few resorts:

Ax-Bonascre This is one of the first resorts you come to on the road from Toulouse, and although you cannot rely on the snow at this height, it is popular for its natural hot springs. Take the RN20 road.

Goulier Neige One of the higher ski resorts, reaching 1,900 m at its peaks. You'll find a good variety of green, blue and red runs, and there is a (free) snowy playground for children at the foot of the slopes. The resort is 125 km from Toulouse, off the RN20, or 20 km from Tarascon-sur-Ariège railway station.

Guzet Right in the middle of the Ariège valley, this is great for families, with a snow park for children. You also get some pretty steep black runs. Take exit 20 from the A64, towards Saint-Girons.

Cauterets Well established ski village and popular with young skiers, so the nightlife is more promising here. You approach the slopes by cable car, and there are plenty of non-ski activities, from spas and bowling alleys to ice rinks and late night bars.

Ariège Aventure

In the middle of the Orlu leisure park, with canoein
and tree climbing for children and adults. Six adven
one canyon. ⓐ Les Forges d'Orlu, Orlu ☏ (05) 61 05 97 33
ⓦ www.ariege-aventure.com 🕐 10.00–19.00 July–Sept;
13.00–18.00, Apr–Jun, Oct & Nov; on advance booking only
(min 12 people), Dec–Mar. Admission charge

Ariège valley

Ariège is a picturesque river that flows through the Pyrénées.
The main town is Foix, in the foothills, with a large castle that
dominates the surrounding scenery.

Pic du Midi de Bigorre

It is worth the slightly longer drive up into the Vallée des Gaves
(Valley of the Mountain Streams) to see one of the Pyrénées' most
stirring sights. It is reached by a modern cable car, or by the previous
option, a four hour hike. ☏ (08) 25 00 28 77 🕐 Daily June–Sept;
Thur–Mon, Oct–May; times vary so call to check. Charge for cable car

Tarascon-sur-Ariège

An attractive town with good restaurants, and the centre for
many prehistoric remains in the area. Its Prehistoric Art Park
shows how water created the limestone caves that people
lived in, how the cave dwellers survived and made tools, and
how and why the wall paintings were created. There are good
walking tours around the park and children get to try their
hand at spear throwing. Booking required. ☏ (05) 61 05 88 37
ⓦ www.ariege.com. Admission charge

CULTURE

La Ferme Basque

Get an idea of how people still live in these rural areas at this lovely farm, which has the added bonus of a fantastic view. Try *brebis*, cheese made from local ewes' milk. Also serves food. ⓐ Route du Cambasque, Cauterets ① (05) 62 92 54 32 ⓦ www.fermebasque.com ① Farm: 10.00–19.00, times flexible. Food served 12.30–14.00, 19.00–20.30, later in July–Aug

La Grotte du Mas d'Azil

On the banks of the L'Arize river, this huge underground complex is accessed via a natural tunnel and used to be the sheltering place of mammoths and rhinoceroses. There's a light and sound show in the caves, a museum and a third-century monolithic chapel. ⓐ Le Mas d'Azil ① (05) 61 69 97 71 ⓦ www.sesta.fr ① 14.00–18.00 April & May; 10.00–12.00, 14.00–18.00 Jun; 10.00–18.00 July & Aug; 14.00–18.00 Sun only, Sept & Oct; 14.00–18.00 Sun only, Mar. Admission charge ① Museum hours vary; see website for details

La Grotte de Niaux

A 12,000 year old cave with detailed pictures of animals that were hunted, and images of stick people tracking them. Enormously popular and places are strictly limited, so book this in advance from the Maison du Midi Pyrénées office in Toulouse (see page 135). ⓐ Niaux ① (05) 61 05 88 28 ⓦ www.niaux.net ① 11 visits per day in July and August. Two in English: 09.00 and 12.30. Times vary. Admission charge

TAKING A BREAK & AFTER DARK

Bar des Trois Pics £ Specialising in local ingredients, this is a friendly place. Work up an appetite first with the nearby fishing, rock climbing and mountain biking. ⓐ Moulis ⓣ (05) 61 04 85 49 ⓛ 09.00–23.00 June–Sept; 11.00–23.00 Oct–May

La Mandoline £ A friendly pizzeria that also has a good range of pastas and salads. ⓐ 2 av. Sabart, Tarascon-sur-Ariège ⓣ (05) 61 05 15 75 ⓛ 12.00–14.30, 19.00–22.30

Le Sacca £ After a hard day's skiing or walking around Cauterets, this is a good place to eat fresh, modern French food. ⓐ Hôtel Astérides Sacca, 11 blvd Latapie-Flurin, Cauterets ⓣ (05) 62 92 50 02 ⓦ www.asterides-sacca.com ⓛ 12.00–14.30, 19.00–22.30

La Grange de l'Agouadis £–££ You might find amateur musicians twanging their guitars here, or gathering round the piano. Even without music, you get to enjoy a varied, relaxed menu from pizzas to salads. ⓐ Martine Papaïx, Aulus les Bains ⓣ (05) 61 96 00 72 ⓦ www.agouadis.com ⓛ 10.30–00.00

Le Txoko £–££ In the middle of a lively ski station, this has a restaurant, a pizzeria, a bowling alley and a bar that doubles as a disco during high season. ⓐ 17 av. de Barèges, Esquièze-Sère, Luz St Sauveur ⓣ (05) 62 92 35 57 ⓛ 11.00–00.00 year round, later at weekends during ski season

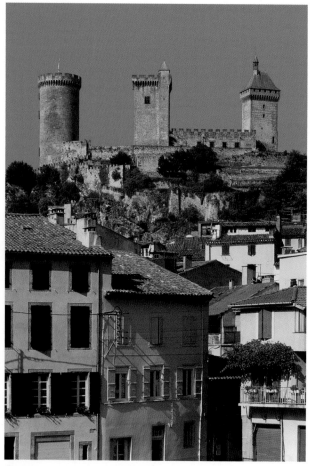

⬤ *Townhouses and Foix's looming castle*

ACCOMMODATION

Ariège valley

Auberge du Mont Calivert £ Pretty restaurant and hotel in the middle of green countryside. ⓐ Bergerat, Montjoie en Courserans ⓣ (05) 61 96 75 22 ⓛ Food served: 12.00–14.00, 19.00–21.30

Hôtel Lons ££ Former coaching inn overlooking the river that runs through the centre of Foix. Popular restaurant also. ⓐ 6 pl. Georges Dutilh, Foix ⓣ (05) 34 09 28 00 ⓦ www.hotel-lons-foix.com ⓛ Food served: 12.00–14.30, 19.00–22.00

Skiing

Hôtel le Breilh £ A simple but well equipped 25 bedroom hotel which makes a good base for hiking in the summer and skiing in the winter. ⓐ Pl. du Breilh, Aix-les-Thermes ⓣ (05) 61 64 24 29 ⓦ www.ariegehotellebreilh.com

Hôtel les Edelweiss £ Very close to the centre of the town and to the ski lift. ⓐ 7 blvd Latapie Flurin, Cauterets ⓣ (05) 62 92 52 75 ⓦ www.edelweiss-hotel.fr

Résidence du Haut Couserans ££ Right at the foot at the ski slopes in Guzet, with a friendly restaurant (with all important central fire), good bar, pool and sauna. ⓐ Guzet 1400,Ustou ⓣ (05) 34 09 09 09 ⓦ www.sbs-vacances.com

The Vineyards

Toulouse is surrounded by vineyards, and visiting them also makes a good excuse to explore some of the pretty towns and villages in the area. Don't attempt them all at once – rather dip in and out on a few day trips. Take your pick from, amongst others, Gaillac, Fronton, Madiran, Côtes de Saint-Mont, Jurançon, Coteaux du Quercy, Tursan, Côtes du Brulhois, Béarn, Pacherenc du Vic-Bilh, Marcillac, Armagnac, Floc de Gascogne. Not all are covered here – there's just too much to see – so instead we have highlighted a few particularly pretty towns in Tarn that allow easy access to the surrounding vines and other activities. For walking, mountain biking and some lake swimming, the Tarn valley itself is beautiful.

GETTING THERE

By rail
Albi is one hour away from Toulouse by train. Trains leave Toulouse central railway station approximately once every hour during the week, and regularly at weekends. The last train from Toulouse to Albi leaves around 22.45. Services are subject to alterations, so always check times beforehand. ⓦ www.sncf.com

By road
Albi is around 90 minutes from Toulouse by car, taking the A68 road to the northeast of the city. Gaillac is much closer, just 50 km northeast of Toulouse on the A89 road, taking around 60 minutes by car. Even closer, just a short hop on the A62 towards Bordeaux, is Fronton.

▲ Spectacular Millau Viaduct, the world's tallest vehicular bridge

There are three buses to and from Toulouse daily, and the journey takes around 90 minutes.

Albi central bus station a Pl. Stalingrad, Albi ☎ (05) 63 54 58 61

Tarnbus (a Rue Hôtel de Ville, Albi ☎ (05) 63 38 43 43) operates a local bus service around Albi and surrounding areas.

SIGHTS & ATTRACTIONS

Albi

Albi is the capital of the Tarn region, an attractive town with a cathedral, good restaurants and wide streets. The entire place is rich in architectural history, and built in Languedoc-style red

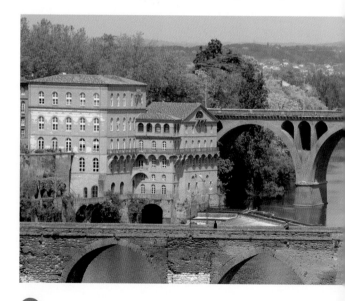

brick, as is Toulouse. Besides its cathedral, Albi is best known as the birth place of the painter Toulouse Lautrec, and you should expect – besides the excellent museum – many of its bars and restaurants to feature frescoes of Moulin Rouge dancers. Many restaurants also offer versions of dishes created by Lautrec, as he was a keen amateur chef.

Information on many of the sights, attractions and events listed here is given by the **Albi tourist office** (🅐 Pl. Ste Cécile, Albi ⓣ (05) 63 49 48 98 ⓦ www.albi-tourisme.com). See also the Town Hall website ⓦ www.mairie-albi.fr.

🔻 *Medieval Pont Vieux, crossing the river at Albi*

Albi grand prix racing

In September every year, Albi gives itself over to race fever. Contact the tourist office (see page 117) for information.

Boat trips

You can take trips along the Tarn river in the flat-bottomed *gabare* boats that traditionally took the wine upriver to Bordeaux for distribution. ⓐ Chalet Albi Croisières (beneath the Palais de la Berbie), Albi ⓣ (05) 63 43 59 63 ⓦ www.albi-croisieres.com ⓛ Trips at 11.00, 11.45, 14.00–18.00, June–Sept. Admission charge

Cathédrale Ste Cécile

This huge cathedral is built like a fortress, imposing itself over the surrounding city with its expanse of red brick and night-time

🔺 *Cordes-sur-Ciel in the Cerou valley*

illumination. Inside it is full of delicate Renaissance paintings, beautiful carved screens and huge stained glass windows. It is worth paying the small charge to see the frescoes.
ⓐ Pl. Ste Cécile, Albi ⓛ 08.30–18.45 June–Sept; 09.00–2.00, 14.00–18.30 Oct–May. Admission charge for Grand Choeur

Cordes-sur-Ciel

This medieval bastide is one of the prettiest villages in France, set high above the surrounding countryside – as the name suggests, it is floating in the clouds. Here they make a dry white, lightly sparkling Perlé wine, which takes its distinctive flavour from the surrounding limestone-soaked vineyards. Other medieval bastides, while you're in the area, include Castelnau-de-Montmiral, Puycelci and Penne.

Domaine Le Roc

A friendly welcome is almost always extended at this family-run château, even during fraught times such as harvest. You should book during the week, but can just turn up at weekends during opening hours. ⓐ 61 route de Toulouse, Fronton ⓣ (05) 61 82 93 90 ⓦ www.leroc-fronton.com ⓛ 10.00–12.00, 14.00–18.00

Fronton

The Côtes de Frontonnais is seen as Toulouse's local wine. This area is also known as the orchard of France, so make sure you pick up lots of local fruit for picnics. Especially good are the chasselas grapes, and the ripe, fragrant peaches. Also worth seeking out is Le Montauriol de Montauban, a delicious chocolate speciality from the nearby town of Montauban.

WINE ROUTE AND FESTIVAL

The beautiful wine town of Gaillac has large cobbled squares, elegant bridges over the river Tarn, and a very attractive *Maison des Vins* set in the beautiful surroundings of the Château de Foucard. Throughout the summer, music and tastings are held in the courtyard every Friday evening. For one weekend in August, the *Maison* gives itself over to a festival of wine in celebration of the town's history of wine making, which dates back to the 1st century. ⓐ Abbaye St Michel, Gaillac ⓣ (05) 63 57 15 40 ⓦ www.vins-gaillac.com ⓛ 10.00–12.00, 14.00–18.00 Mon–Sat

The town also has a well-organised and signed wine route full of welcoming characters. A few particularly good wine makers to visit are:

Robert Plageoles A local legend, with the complete library of traditional local grape varieties. He has rediscovered some that almost disappeared years ago. Ask for a sample of his wines made from grapes dried on straw mats. ⓐ Domaine des Tres Cantous, Cahuzac sur Vère ⓣ (05) 63 33 90 40 ⓦ www.vins-plageoles.com ⓛ 08.00–12.00, 14.00–18.00 Mon–Fri

Alain Rotier A dynamic young wine maker who speaks great English and knows the area intimately. His Cuvée Renaissance gets consistent plaudits, and he's full of good suggestions for where to eat and drink. ⓐ Petit Nareye, Cadalen, Gaillac ⓣ (05) 63 41 75 14 ⓦ www.domaine-rotier.com ⓛ 08.00–12.00, 14.00–19.00 Mon–Sat ⓐ A68 exit 10, follow signs direct to the Domaine

Information on sights, attractions and events in Fronton is available from the Town Hall. ⓐ 1 esplanade Marcorelle, Fronton ⓣ (05) 62 79 92 92 ⓦ www.mairie-fronton.fr

Golf Albi-Lasbordes

An 18-hole golf course with a good restaurant and bar.
ⓐ Chemin Las Bordes, Albi ⓣ (05) 63 54 98 07 ⓦ www.golfalbi.com
ⓛ 08.30–18.30. Admission charge

Jardin des Paradis

A contemporary, Japanese-inspired garden in the middle of Cordes-sur-Ciel with a lovely mix of flowers, vegetation and quiet meditative corners. ⓐ Pl. du Théron, Cordes-sur-Ciel ⓣ (05) 63 56 29 77 ⓦ www.jardindesparadis.eu ⓦ 14.00–18.00 Apr–mid-June, Sept & Oct; 10.00–19.00 mid-June–Aug. Admission charge, under 8s free

Millau Viaduct

If you've got a head for heights, don't miss Sir Norman Foster's Millau Viaduct, crossing the Tarn River gorge in the Cevennes national park. This is slightly further away from Toulouse (at least a 2.5 hour drive) but is spectacular.

Pont Vieux

An eyeglass bridge over the Tarn River that has been in existence since 1035. A perfect photo spot.

CULTURE

Albi jazz & classical music festivals

June sees a popular jazz festival in Albi, with events all over the town. A classical music festival is held over the last two weeks of July. Contact the tourist office for information.

Musée des Beaux-Arts

Wide-ranging exhibits from contemporary sculptures to romantic painters. ⓐ Château de Foucard, Av. Dom Vayssette, Gaillac ⓣ (05) 63 57 18 25 ⓦ www.ville-gaillac.fr ⓛ 10.00–12.00, 14.00–18.00 Wed–Mon, Apr–Oct; 10.00–12.00, 14.00–18.00 Fri–Sun, Nov–Mar. Admission charge

Rando'Jazz

October in Fronton sees a mix of walking and music with this unusual jazz festival. Most of the venues are within easy walking distance. Contact the Town Hall for more information (see page 117).

Saveurs et Senteurs du Frontonnais (Food & Flavours of Fronton)

A big festival is held in Fronton on the last weekend of August. There's jazz and blues to keep you entertained and local producers of everything from *foie gras* to honey. Contact the Town Hall (see page 117) for more information.

Toulouse Lautrec Museum

Lautrec was born in Albi and this museum contains over 500 examples of his work, from early pencil sketches right up to his famous Paris brothel scenes. ⓐ Palais de la Berbie, pl. Ste Cécile, Albi ☎ (05) 63 49 48 70 🕐 09.00–18.00, July & Aug; 10.00–12.00, 14.00–18.00, Sept–June. Admission charge

TAKING A BREAK & AFTER DARK

See also Accommodation section on page 124.

La Calèche £ Among the French bistro classics you'll find a few good vegetarian platters. ⓐ 6 rue de la Piale, Albi ☎ (05) 63 54 15 52 🕐 12.00–14.00, 19.30–22.30

Le Grand Pontié £ Large and airy, with a brasserie downstairs, pizzeria upstairs, and pavement café outside. Good view overlooking the main square. ⓐ Pl. du Vigan, Albi ☎ (05) 63 54 16 34 ⓔ cafelepontie@wanadoo.fr 🕐 12.00–14.00, 19.00–23.30

La Falaise ££ Lovely outside courtyard at this restaurant in the heart of the Gaillac wine routes, where you can eat beneath huge old trees. ⓐ Routes de Cordes, Cahuzac-sur-Vère ☎ (05) 63 33 96 31 ⓦ www.lafalaiserestaurant.com 🕐 12.00–14.00, 19.30–22.30 Tues–Sun

Chateau de Salettes ££–£££ Located in a gorgeous building dating from the 13th century, this is a great place to stop for a bite of lunch or dinner. ⓐ Lieu dit Salettes, Cahuzac sur Vère ☎ (05) 63 33 60 60 ⓦ www.chateaudesalettes.com 🕐 12.00–13.00, 19.30–21.30

L'Epicurien £££ Worth its reputation, this is a stylish restaurant with good quality ingredients and a small, focused menu. Fun

ideas for children also, like special tasting menus. ⓐ 42 pl. Jean
Jaurès, Albi ⓣ (05) 63 53 10 70 ⓦ www.restaurantlepicurien.com
ⓛ 12.00–14.00, 20.00–22.30 Tues–Sat

ACCOMMODATION

Camping Le Caussels £ Just a few miles outside of Millau, this
very basic campsite makes a good base for exploring the region
if you don't mind roughing it for a day or two. ⓐ Val de Caussels,
Route de Millau, Albi ⓣ (05) 63 60 37 06 ⓛ Apr–Oct
ⓝ Bus: 5 from Place du Vigan

La Regence George V £ Friendly hotel with good sized rooms,
near to the bus and railway stations. ⓐ 27-29 av Maréchal Joffre,
Albi ⓣ (05) 63 54 24 16 ⓦ www.hotelgeorgev.com

Hôtel-Restaurant de Vieil Alby ££ Small, good value rooms
at this very central hotel, but what really swings it here is
the restaurant, where you can eat fantastic seasonal food.
ⓐ 25 rue Henri de Toulouse Lautrec, Albi ⓣ (05) 63 54 14 69
ⓦ www.levieilalby.com

Le Manoir de Raynaudes ££–£££ Out in the Tarn countryside, this
secluded and very charming country house hotel is renowned for
its food (in fact, a book was written about it, *A Table in the Tarn*).
About half an hour from Albi. ⓐ Monestiès ⓣ (05) 63 36 91 90
ⓦ www.raynaudes.com

ⓞ *Le Pont Saint Pierre*

PRACTICAL
information

Directory

GETTING THERE

By air

Toulouse Blagnac Airport (see page 48) is served by many UK and Irish airlines, including British Airways, BMI and Aer Lingus. The flight time from London is approximately 90 minutes.

Air France ☎ 08 20 82 08 20 🌐 www.airfrance.fr

EasyJet ☎ 08 25 08 25 08 🌐 www.easyjet.com

Aer Lingus ☎ 01 70 20 00 72 🌐 www.aerlingus.ie

British Airways ☎ 08 25 82 54 00 🌐 www.britishairways.com

BMI ☎ 01 41 91 87 04 🌐 www.bmibaby.com

Many people are aware that air travel emits CO_2, which contributes to climate change. You may be interested in the possibility of lessening the environmental impact of your flight through **Climate Care** (🌐 www.climatecare.org), which offsets your CO_2 by funding environmental projects around the world.

By rail

To get from London to Toulouse by rail, take the Eurostar to Paris and then change to a TGV from Paris to Toulouse. The trip should take about ten hours, and trains run regularly throughout the day. Return fares are often very good value.

Eurostar for cross-Channel trains ☎ (08705) 186 186 🌐 www.eurostar.com

SNCF for trains within France ☎ (08) 92 35 35 35 🌐 www.voyages-sncf.com

Thomas Cook European Rail Timetable ☎ (01733) 416 477 🌐 www.thomascookpublishing.com

By road

The A62 motorway runs south from Bordeaux to Toulouse, carrying on south to Carcassonne and Montpellier. The journey from Bordeaux to Toulouse takes between two and three hours. The A1 goes from Paris to Toulouse, with an average driving time of around eight hours. It is just about possible to drive from the UK to Toulouse, via Calais, in one day, but not recommended.

● *The TGV brings Toulouse within easy reach of Paris*

Remember to bring both parts of your driving licence and to inform your insurance company before driving to France. You should carry a copy of your valid insurance certificate.

When you are in the region, information on traffic is available on ❶ (05) 61 22 29 22

Eurolines (Ⓦ www.eurolines.com) is Europe's largest coach operator, serving all of France.

ENTRY FORMALITIES

EU citizens can travel to France without a visa. For citizens of the USA, Canada, Australia, New Zealand and South Africa, visits of up to three months do not require a visa. Visitors from other countries do require a visa. All visitors need a passport.

EU citizens may bring into France personal possessions and goods for personal use, provided they have been bought in the EU. For full regulations visit Ⓦ www.douane.gouv.fr

Animals entering France need a European (EU) Pet Passport. This is a booklet which contains all the relevant information about your pet, including an identification number and proof of a valid vaccine against the rabies virus. Animals travelling within any European Union countries other than Ireland, Sweden, Malta and the United Kingdom also need to have identification by microchip or tattoo. Tattoos are only acceptable until July 2011. All vets should have the relevant information and be able to get your animal ready for travelling with you.

MONEY

The currency of France is the euro (€). 1 euro = 100 cents (also called eurocents). Euros come in notes of €5, €10, €20, €50, €100,

€200, €500. Coins are in denominations of €1 and €2, and in cents worth 1c, 2c, 5c, 10c, 20c and 50c. For current exchange rates, check www.travelex.com or www.oanda.com

ATM machines are plentiful in Toulouse and are the easiest way to withdraw money while in the city. Traveller's cheques and foreign money can be cashed at most banks, bureaux de change and some hotels. You will need your passport as identification. Major international credit cards are accepted in most large stores and restaurants and in ATM machines.

A 15 per cent service charge is usually included in the bill in French restaurants, although often not in cafés. It is customary to add another 2–3 per cent on top if the service has been good, or to round the bill up to the nearest euro. Taxi drivers expect 10 per cent of the fare on top, and hairdressers around the same. When staying in hotels, it is usual to tip staff a few euros for carrying baggage to rooms.

HEALTH, SAFETY & CRIME

Tap water is safe to drink, and many public parks have drinking fountains. *Eau Non Potable* means the water is not safe to drink. At almost all restaurants, you will be given a *pichet d'eau* (jug of tap water) when you sit down.

No inoculations are necessary for British citizens travelling to France. If you have any queries, ask your doctor before leaving, pick up the Department of Health leaflet T5 'Health Advice for Travellers' from a post office, or visit the travel advice section of ⓦ www.dh.gov.uk.

It is always advisable to take a small first aid kit with you, and to keep it in the car if you are travelling around. If you take regular medication take enough for your holiday, and you should consider packing your regular headache remedy. If travelling in summer, remember to take sun cream.

As in any big city, be careful of valuables, watch for pickpockets and lock your car and belongings up securely. At night, avoid the areas around the central railway station and between rue Bayard and allées Jean Jaurès, as well as the Boulevards. Be aware that there are a number of homeless people and beggars in Toulouse.

OPENING HOURS

Banks are generally open 09.00–12.30, 14.00 or 14.30–16.30 or 17.00 Monday to Friday. Shops open 09.30 or 10.00–12.30, 14.00–19.00 Monday to Saturday, with some remaining open over lunch and very few (except bakeries) opening on Sundays. Standard opening hours for pharmacies are 08.30 or 09.00–12.00, 14.00–19.00 Monday to Saturday. For an after-hours pharmacy, see page 137. Restaurants generally serve food 12.00–14.00, 19.00–22.30, with some closing on Mondays and others remaining open throughout the day.

TOILETS

There are public toilets at several places in the centre of Toulouse and most are clean and well maintained. There are separate ones for men and women, and most will have an entrance fee. The airport and the railway station both have good public toilets, and most museums are also a good bet for clean facilities.

CHILDREN

Toulouse is a very child-friendly city, and small children are welcomed in almost all hotels, cafés and restaurants. Pharmacies sell nappies and baby food and all the other essentials. Remember in summer it can get very hot, so even when wandering around the city make sure your children are wearing protective clothing, sun cream and hats.

The city is full of attractions for children, not least the Cité de l'Espace with its IMAX cinema and Little Astronauts play area. Other good bets are:

Centre Régional d'Information Jeunesse Plenty of ideas on how to keep little ones entertained. ⓐ 17 rue de Metz ① (05) 61 21 20 20 ⓦ www.crij.org ⓛ 10.00–18.00 Mon–Fri, 10.00–13.00, 14.00–17.00 Sat ⓜ Metro: Capitole

L'Envers du Décor An interactive theatre show suitable for children from the age of seven. The name means 'behind the scenes' and children in the audience also help put on the show. ⓐ Théâtre Le Fil à Plomb, 30 rue de la Chaîne ① (05) 62 30 99 77 ⓦ http://lefilaplomb.free.fr ⓜ Metro: Capitole

Fondation Bemberg A museum and gallery running several events for children, from brass plate rubbing to story-telling. See page 64 for contact details and opening times.

PlayPark A playground with over 1000 sq m of play space, for children from 0 to 12. ⓐ 18 route de Muret, Portet-sur-Garonne ① (05) 62 87 91 97 ⓦ www.playpark.fr ⓛ 16.00–20.00 Tues, Thur & Fri, 10.00–21.00 Wed, Sat & Sun ⓜ Car: N20 from Toulouse to Portet-sur-Garonne. Admission charge

COMMUNICATIONS

Internet

There are a number of internet cafés around the city, and increasingly hotels and some cafés have wireless zones with either free or paid-for access. The streets around Place du Capitole have a number of small internet cafés that are cheap and cheerful.

Cyber Copie ⓐ 18 rue des Lois ⓣ (05) 61 21 03 73
ⓦ www.cybercopie.fr ⓛ 09.00–19.00 ⓝ Metro: Capitole
Cyber King ⓐ 31 rue Gambetta ⓛ 10.30–22.00 Mon–Sat, 14.00–21.00 Sun ⓝ Metro: Capitole

TELEPHONING TOULOUSE

To call Toulouse from abroad, dial your own international prefix (00 in most countries) then 33 for France. The area code for southwest France, including Toulouse, is 05, followed by a number which is always eight digits in length. When dialling from abroad, drop the first 0, to leave 00 33 5 and the eight-digit number. When dialling Toulouse from anywhere in France, dial 05 and then the eight-digit number.

TELEPHONING ABROAD

To call abroad from France, dial 00 for an international connection, then your own country code, then the area code and phone number you desire leaving out the initial '0'. Some useful country codes include: UK 44, Republic of Ireland 353, USA and Canada 1, Australia 61, New Zealand 64, and South Africa 27.

Phone

Card-operated public phone boxes are available across Toulouse.
You can buy a *télécarte* (phone card) at a *tabac* (newsagent).
For Directory Enquires call ➊ 118 712 from any phone.

Post

There are over 25 post offices throughout downtown Toulouse.
Post offices sell telephone cards, and usually have photocopiers
or a fax machine available for public use. Most post offices have
coin-operated machines for buying stamps and weighing
packages if you don't want to wait in line.

Post boxes are yellow and easy to spot. Stamps can be bought
either from the post office or from a *tabac* (newsagents).

The main post office in Toulouse is very close to Place du
Capitole. ➌ 9 rue Lafayette ➊ (05) 61 33 40 00 ⓦ www.laposte.fr
🕐 08.00–19.00 Mon–Fri, 08.00–12.00 Sat Ⓝ Metro Capitole

ELECTRICITY

France runs on 220 volts with 2-pin plugs. British appliances will
need an adaptor, easily obtained from any electrical or hardware
store, or from the airport. US and other equipment designed for
110 volts will need a transformer.

TRAVELLERS WITH DISABILITIES

Toulouse airport and railway stations have good access points
for travellers who need extra assistance, and there are lifts in
all the metro stations and most of the larger hotels. However,
buses tend to be ill-equipped, and there are many hotels which
do not have bathrooms and bedrooms that are easily adapted

...irs. Useful organisations for information and
...ude:

RADA... ...he principal UK forum and pressure group for people
with disabilities. ⓐ 12 City Forum, 250 City Road, London EC1V 8AF
ⓣ (020) 7250 3222 ⓦ www.radar.org.uk

SATH (Society for Accessible Travel & Hospitality) Advises
US-based travellers with disabilities. ⓐ 347 Fifth Ave,
Suite 605, New York 10016 ⓣ (212) 447 7284 ⓦ www.sath.org

**Association des Paralysés en France Délégation Départementale
des Alpes-Maritimes** ⓐ 21 blvd Mantéga Righi, 06100 Nice
ⓣ (04) 92 15 78 70 ⓦ www.apf.asso.fr

TOURIST INFORMATION

To reach any tourist board in France, dial 3264 and clearly say
the name of the town or city you are interested in. You will be
put through automatically to the correct tourist office. Calls
cost 34 cents per min.

Maison de La France (French Tourist Board) has a UK branch
that can offer plenty of info before you leave. ⓐ 178 Piccadilly,
W1J 9AL London ⓣ 09068 244 123 (calls cost 60p per min)
ⓦ www.franceguide.com

Office de Tourisme de Toulouse is the main tourist office
in Toulouse. It is housed in a 16th-century tower and former
dungeon, making it something of an attraction in itself.
ⓐ Square du Général Charles de Gaulle ⓣ (05) 61 11 02 22
ⓦ www.toulouse-tourisme.com ⓛ 09.00–18.00 Mon–Fri,
09.00–12.30, 14.00–18.00 Sat, 10.00–12.30 14–17.00 Sun,
Oct–May; 09.00–19.00 Mon–Sat, 10.30–17.15 Sun, June–Sept
ⓝ Metro: Capitole

Maison du Midi Pyrénées (Comité Régional du Tourisme Midi-Pyrénées) ⓐ 54 blvd de l'Embouchure ⓣ (05) 61 13 55 55 ⓦ www.tourisme-midi-pyrenees.com ⓝ Metro: Capitole

BACKGROUND READING

Last Tango in Toulouse by Mary Moody. Set in the countryside around Toulouse, this looks at what happens when a gardening writer gives it all up to start again in southwest France and embarks on an affair.

Le Petit Prince (The Little Prince) by Antoine de Saint Exupéry. A classic. Any books by the same author can get you in the mood for a trip to Toulouse.

Wines of Southwest France by Paul Strang. A good overview of the treasures that can be found in the area.

Emergencies

The following are emergency free-call numbers:

Ambulance ☎ 15

Fire ☎ 18

Police ☎ 17

All emergency services from a mobile phone ☎ 112

Note that in France, *pompiers* (firemen) also deal with first aid and most other emergency situations.

MEDICAL SERVICES

Visitors from the UK require a European Health Insurance Card (EHIC), which guarantees emergency treatment.

Emergency doctors

SOS Médecins (day) ☎ (05) 61 33 00 00

SOS Médecin de garde (night) ☎ (05) 61 49 66 66 or (05) 61 22 00 00

See ⓦ www.sosmedecins-france.fr

English-speaking dentists

Dr Nicole Garbasky @ 45 allées Jean Jaurès ☎ (05) 61 62 30 58

Dr Jean Michel @ 135 route de Seilh, Aussonne ☎ (05) 61 85 14 19

Hospitals

CHR Rangueil @ Av. Jean Poulhes ☎ (05) 61 32 25 33

CHR Purpan @ Pl. du Docteur Baylac ☎ (05) 61 77 22 33

Hôpital Larrey @ 24 chemin de Pouvourville ☎ (05) 67 77 14 33

Hôpital des Enfants (children's hospital) @ 330 av. de Grande Bretagne ☎ (05) 34 55 86 33

After-hours pharmacy ⓐ 70–76 allées Jean Jaurès
ⓣ (05) 61 62 38 05 ⓒ 20.00–08.00 Mon–Sat,
20.00–09.00 Sun and public holidays
Centre Anti-Poisons (Poison Centre) ⓣ (05) 61 49 33 33
Urgence Vétérinaire (Emergency Vet) ⓣ (05) 61 11 21 31

POLICE
Hôtel de Police (main police headquarters)
ⓐ 23 blvd de l'Embouchure ⓣ (05) 61 12 77 77
Lost Property ⓐ 17 pl. Saint Cyprien ⓣ (05) 62 27 63 00

EMBASSIES & CONSULATES
Australia ⓐ 4 rue Jean Rey, Paris ⓣ (01) 40 59 33 01
Canada ⓐ 10 rue Jules de Rességuier, Toulouse ⓣ (05) 61 52 19 06
Ireland ⓐ 4 rue Rude, Paris ⓣ (01) 44 17 67 67
New Zealand ⓐ 7 ter, rue Leonard de Vinci, Paris ⓣ (01) 45 00 24 11
South Africa ⓐ 59 quai d'Orsay, Paris ⓣ (01) 53 59 23 23
UK ⓐ 353 blvd Wilson, Bordeaux ⓣ (05) 57 22 21 10
US ⓐ 25 allées Jean Jaurès, Toulouse ⓣ (05) 34 41 36 50

EMERGENCY PHRASES

Help!   Au secours!   *Or secoors!*

Call the police/fire service/ambulance!
Appelez la police/les pompiers/un ambulance!
Appeley la police/leh pompee-eh/un ambulance!

A

Abattoirs, Les 79
accommodation 36–9
  Pyrénées 113
  Vineyards 124
Aeronautical Toulouse
  12–13, 86
Aerothèque 86
Ailes Anciennes 86
air travel 48, 126
Albi 116–17, 122
Amphithéâtre Romain
  de Purpan 86–7
Andorra 106–7
Archives Municipales 94
Ariège Aventure 109
Ariège Valley 109
Arnaud-Bernard 87
arts see culture

B

background reading 135
bars & clubs 30–3
  see also nightlife
Basilisque Saint Sernin 58
bicycle hire 34
boat trips 49, 56, 118
Botanical Garden 62–3
Boulevards 86–100
bus travel 48–9, 53,
  103–6, 114–16, 128

C

cafés
  Boulevards &
    further afield 98

Île Ramier &
  the Left Bank 84
Old Town 70
Pyrénées 111
Vineyards 123–4
Café Théâtre
  Les Minimes 94
Canal du Midi 16
Capitole 58–62
car hire 56
casinos 33, 75, 100
cassoulet 27
Cathédrale Paroisse
  Saint Etienne 62
Cathédrale
  Ste Cécile 118–19
Centre de Congrès
  Pierre Baudis 90
Centre Municipal de
  l'Affiche, de la Carte
  Postale et de l'Art
  Graphique 80
Chapelle des
  Carmélites 62
Chapelle St Christophe 75
children 1301
cinemas 33, 46, 63
Cinémathèque 63
Cité de l'Espace 90
climate 8
Cordes-sur-Ciel 119
crime 129–30
culture 18–20
customs & duty 107, 128

D

dance 8, 10
disabled travellers 133–4
Domaine le Roc 119
Dôme de la Grave 75
driving 48–9, 56, 103, 114,
  127–8

E

EDF Bazacle 63
Église Nôtre Dame
  de la Daurade 62
Église Saint Aubin 90
Église Saint Nicolas
  de la Grave 90
Église Saint Pierre
  des Cuisines 64
electricity 133
embassies &
  consulates 137
emergencies 136–7
entertainment 30–3
  see also nightlife
L'Envers du Décor 131
Espace Croix Baragnon 64
Espace Saint-Cyprien 80–1
events & festivals 8–11, 122
Exhibition Centre 78

F

Ferme Basque 110
film 33
Fondation Bemberg 64, 131
food & drink 24–9

Food & Flavours
    of Fronton 122
football 34
Fronton 119–22

G

Galerie du
    Château d'Eau 81
Galerie de la Halle
    aux Poissons 64
Gaillac 120
Garonne 74
Golf Albi-Lasbordes 121
graffiti art 20, 45
Grand Prix 118
Grand Rond 62–3
Grotte du Mas d'Azil 110
Grotte de Niaux 110

H

Halle aux Graines 94–5
health 129–30, 136–7
Hippodrome
    de la Cepière 75–8
history 14–15
Hôtel d'Assézat 64
Hôtel Dieu
    Saint Jacques 78
hotels *see*
    accommodation

I

Île Ramier &
    the Left Bank 74–85
Instituto Cervantes 95
internet 132

J

Jardin Compans
    Caffarelli 91
Jardin des Paradis 121
Jardin des Plantes 62–3
Jardin Raymond VI 78
Jolimont
    Observatoire 91–2

L

language 23, 28, 49, 137
lifestyle 16–17
listings 30

M

M J C Roguet 81
markets 10, 45, 68, 83, 98
Médiathèque
    José Cabanis 95
metro 53
Millau Viaduct 121
money 128–9
Musée des Augustins 66
Musée des Beaux-Arts 122
Musée Georges Labit 95–6
Musée de la Medicine 81
Musée Paul Dupuy 66
Musée de la Résistance
    et de la Déportation 96
Musée Saint Raymond 66
Musée du
    Vieux Toulouse 66–7
music 18, 94–5, 122

N

nightlife 30–3

Boulevards &
    further afield 98–100
Île Ramier &
    the Left Bank 84–5
Old Town 70–3
Pyrénées 111
Vineyards 123–4

O

Old Town 58–73
opening hours 130

P

Parc des Expositions 78
Parc Fontaine Lestang 79
Parc du Ramier 79
parks and gardens 91
passports & visas 128
Péniche Maison
    de la Violette 92
phone 132–3
Pic du Midi de Bigorre 109
Place de la Daurade 63
PlayPark 131
police 137
Pont Neuf 42
Pont Vieux 121
post 133
Prairie des Filtres 79
public holidays 11
public transport 48–9, 53,
    102–6, 114–16, 126, 128
Pyrénées 102–13

INDEX

R

rail travel 48, 53, 102–3,
  114, 126–7
Rando'Jazz 122
restaurants 27–8
  Boulevards &
    further afield 98–100
  Île Ramier &
    the Left Bank 84–5
  Old Town 70–2
  Pyrénées 111
  Vineyards 123–4
rugby 34

S

safety 129–30
Saveurs et Senteurs
  du Frontonnais 122
seasons 8

shopping 22–3
  Boulevards &
    further afield 97–8
  Île Ramier &
    the Left Bank 82–3
  Old Town 67–9
Site Airbus &
  Clement Adler 92
skiing 108
sport & activities 34–5
symbols &
  abbreviations 4

T

Tarascon-sur-Ariège 109
Tarn region 114–25
taxis 56
theatre 9–10, 30, 82, 94
Théâtre du Capitole 18

Théâtre Garonne 82
time difference 48
tipping 28, 129
toilets 130
Touch and Go 94
Toulouse Lautrec
  Museum 122–3
tourist information 134–5
Train Jaune 102–3
tram 53

V

Vineyards 114–25
Violet House Barge 92

W

weather 8, 46–7
wine route & festival 120

Y

Yellow Train 102–3

Editorial/project management: Lisa Plumridge
Copy editor: Monica Guy
Layout/DTP: Alison Rayner

The publishers would like to thank the following individuals and organisations for supplying their copyright photographs for this book: Airbus, page 87; BigStockPhoto.com (Paolo Baruchello, page 103; Claudio Giovanni Colombo, page 101; David Hughes, page 112; Fedor Patrakov, pages 106–7; Sybille Yates, page 21); Fotolia.com (Jerome Berdoulat, page 19; ComlaCom, page 25; Joerg Gamroth, page 15; Loic Le Brusq/Fotolia.com, page 32); iStockphoto.com (Jasmin Awad, page 83; Patrick Barlet, pages 74–5; Jean-Yves Benedeyt, pages 21, 57 & 59; Fred Challis, page 118; Jacques Croizer, pages 116–17; Guillaume Dubé, pages 5, 31, 40–1 & 99; Marco Kopp, pages 12–13; Monika Lewandowska, page 115; Andrew Lewis, page 93); X Marchant/Stockxpert.com, page 9; SXU.hu (Christopher Grondahl, page 29; Kiril Havezov, page 52;

Send your thoughts to
books@thomascook.com

- **Found a great bar, club, shop or must-see sight that we don't feature?**
- **Like to tip us off about any information that needs a little updating?**
- **Want to tell us what you love about this handy little guidebook and more importantly how we can make it even handier?**

Then here's your chance to tell all! Send us ideas, discoveries and recommendations today and then look out for your valuable input in the next edition of this title.

Email the above address (stating the title) or write to: pocket guides Series Editor, Thomas Cook Publishing, PO Box 227, Coningsby Road, Peterborough PE3 8SB, UK.

WHAT'S IN YOUR GUIDEBOOK?

Independent authors Impartial up-to-date information from our travel experts who meticulously source local knowledge.

Experience Thomas Cook's 165 years in the travel industry and guidebook publishing enriches every word with expertise you can trust.

Travel know-how Thomas Cook has thousands of staff working around the globe, all living and breathing travel.

Editors Travel-publishing professionals, pulling everything together to craft a perfect blend of words, pictures, maps and design.

You, the traveller We deliver a practical, no-nonsense approach to information, geared to how you really use it.

Csongor Varga/SXC.hu, page 127); Ville de Toulouse, pages 6, 17, 35, 39, 43, 44, 47, 65, 67, 71, 80, 96, 125.

ABOUT THE AUTHOR

Jane Anson is a writer and columnist, based in Bordeaux, France – just two hours from Toulouse – and the author of Thomas Cook's HotSpot *Corsica* and CitySpot *Bordeaux* guidebooks. She also writes widely for the *Telegraph*, the *Irish Independent*, *Food & Travel*, *Gourmet Traveller* and *Wine & Spirit* magazines, plus a number of other international publications.

Useful phrases

English	French	Approx pronunciation
BASICS		
Yes	Oui	*Wee*
No	Non	*Nawng*
Please	S'il vous plaît	*Sylvooplay*
Thank you	Merci	*Mehrsee*
Hello	Bonjour	*Bawngzhoor*
Goodbye	Au revoir	*Aw revwahr*
Excuse me	Excusez-moi	*Ekskewzeh-mwah*
Sorry	Désolé(e)	*Dehzoleh*
That's okay	Ça va	*Sahr vahr*
I don't speak French	Je ne parle pas français	*Zher ner pahrl pah frahngsay*
Do you speak English?	Parlez-vous anglais?	*Pahrlay-voo ohnglay?*
Good morning	Bonjour	*Bawng-zhoor*
Good afternoon	Bonjour	*Bawng-zhoor*
Good evening	Bonsoir	*Bawng-swah*
Goodnight	Bonne nuit	*Bun nwee*
My name is ...	Je m'appelle ...	*Zher mahpehl ...*
NUMBERS		
One	Un/Une	*Uhn/Oon*
Two	Deux	*Dur*
Three	Trois	*Trwah*
Four	Quatre	*Kahtr*
Five	Cinq	*Sank*
Six	Six	*Seess*
Seven	Sept	*Seht*
Eight	Huit	*Weet*
Nine	Neuf	*Nurf*
Ten	Dix	*Deess*
Twenty	Vingt	*Vang*
Fifty	Cinquante	*Sangkahnt*
One hundred	Cent	*Sohn*
SIGNS & NOTICES		
Airport	Aéroport	*Ahehrohpohr*
Rail station	Gare	*Gahr*
Platform	Quai	*Kay*
Smoking/ No smoking	Permit de fumer/ Interdit de fumer	*Permee der foom-eh/ Anterdee der foom-eh*
Toilets	Toilettes	*Twahlaitt*
Ladies/Gentlemen	Femmes/Hommes	*Fam/Ommh*
Subway/Bus	Métro/Bus	*Maytroa/Booss*